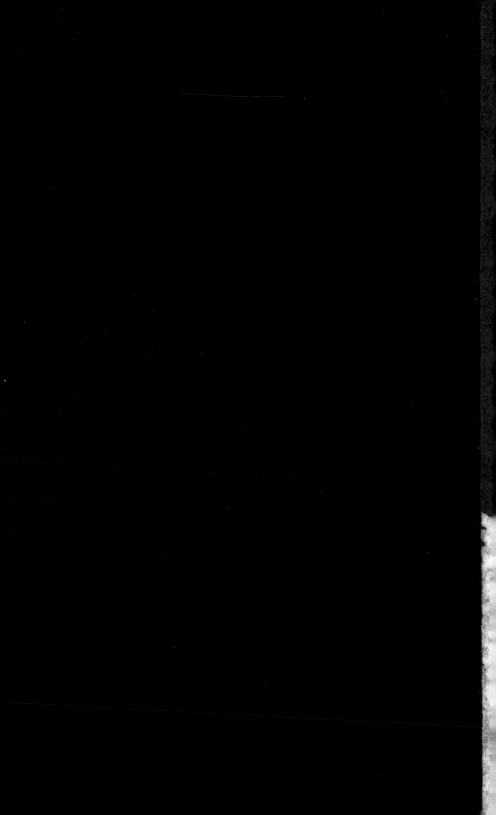

BREAKING THE SILENCE

DAVID IKARD

BREAKING
the Silence

Toward a Black Male Feminist Criticism

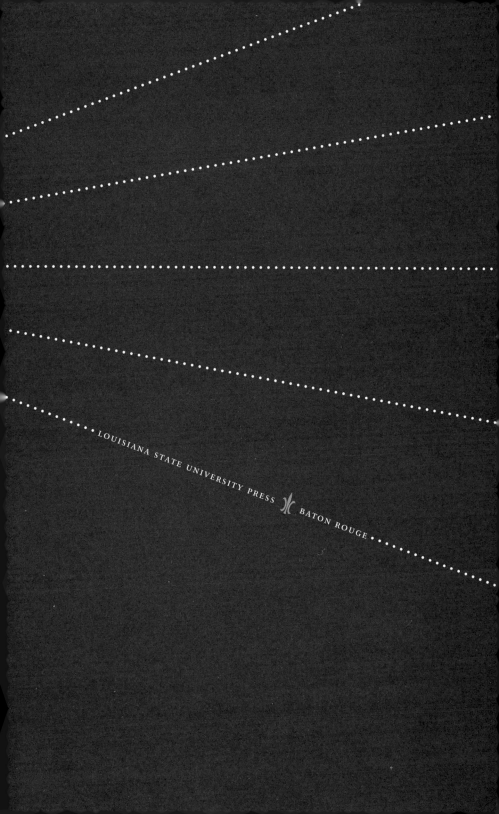

LOUISIANA STATE UNIVERSITY PRESS · BATON ROUGE

Published by Louisiana State University Press
Copyright © 2007 by Louisiana State University Press
All rights reserved
Manufactured in the United States of America
First printing

DESIGNER: Michelle A. Garrod
TYPEFACE: Sabon
PRINTER AND BINDER: Edwards Brothers, Inc.

LIBRARY OF CONGRESS CATALOGING-IN-PUBLICATION DATA
Ikard, David, 1972–
    Breaking the silence : toward a Black male feminist criticism / David Ikard.
        p. cm.
    Includes bibliographical references and index.
    ISBN-13: 978-0-8071-3213-5 (alk. paper)
        1. American fiction—African American authors—History and criticism. 2. African American women in literature. 3. African American men in literature. 4. African American women—Race identity. 5. African American men—Race identity. 6. Sex differences in literature. 7. Suffering in literature. 8. Patriarchy in literature. I. Title.
PS374.N4I53 2007
813.009'896073—dc22

                                                                            2006015764

Portions of chapters 1 and 3, respectively, appeared previously in slightly different form as "Love Jones: A Black Male Feminist Critique of Chester Himes's *If He Hollers Let Him Go*," *African American Review* 36 (Summer 2002): 299–310; and "'So Much of What We Know Ain't So': The Other Gender in Toni Cade Bambara's *The Salt Eaters*," *Obsidian III* 4, no. 1 (Summer 2002): 76–100. Used by permission.

This book is dedicated to my wife and children:
RaMonda (aka Ray Ray, Momma, and Ra), Elijah David,
and Octavia Damali.

Thanks for helping me weather the storms.

Frankly, I want the same thing now that I did thirty years ago when I joined the Civil Rights movement and twenty years ago when I joined the women's movement, came out, and felt more alive than I ever dreamed possible: freedom.

BARBARA SMITH, "Where's the Revolution?"

It began to seem that one would have to hold in the mind forever two ideas which seemed to be in opposition. The first idea was acceptance, the acceptance, totally without rancor, of life as it is, and men as they are: in the light of this idea, it goes without saying that injustice is a commonplace. But this did not mean that one could be complacent, for the second idea was of equal power: that one must never, in one's own life, accept these injustices as commonplace but must fight them with all one's strength. This fight begins, however, in the heart and it now had been laid to my charge to keep my own heart free of hatred and despair.

JAMES BALDWIN, "Notes of a Native Son"

Contents

Acknowledgments

I could not have completed this book without the guidance, support, and love of my family, friends, and mentors. Thanks go to my wacky, fun-loving, and fiercely loyal siblings Randy, Crystal, Regina, Terry, Tiffany, and Baquita (honorary sister). And, to my beautiful and precocious nieces and nephews, JaKayla, Jasmine, Junior, and Tyrell, who are destined for great things. Much love also goes to my dynamic aunts and uncles—Mattie, "Netta," Bettie, Pearl, May, Allen, Michael, and "Woody"—who continue to inspire me to be a better son, father, and husband. My parents are to be especially commended for teaching me to dream big and to strive for excellence in all of my life pursuits. Bombarded with intense racial barriers in the educational arena, they both were unable to finish high school. However, they made sure that their children would not succumb to similar fates. Serving on and heading up PTA boards, volunteering to coach our Little League sport teams, organizing protests and demonstrations at our local schools to ensure that black students received fair treatment, my parents went above and beyond the call of duty to provide us with the best possible opportunities for success. Their efforts paid off. All of us finished high school and most of us went on to college. Personally speaking, I know that their tireless love and support allowed me to overcome the enormous racial obstacles that radically altered the dreams and aspirations of many of our black peers. They deserve the bulk of the credit for preparing me for life and success.

Navigating the tricky political waters of academe is extremely challenging. Fortunately, I have been blessed with a host of mentors that have equipped me with the necessary critical, emotional, and spiritual tools to survive, and even thrive, in this environment. Special thanks go to my second grade teacher Mr. Roseboro, who cultivated my passion for learning and first ignited my desire to go to college; to the late Prof. Edward Clarke, who helped me to demystify whiteness and graduate school; to the late Prof. Doris Laryea, who first turned me on to African American literature; to Prof. Joyce Pettis, who continues to be a wonderful advisor and friend; to Prof. Barbara Baines, who taught me how to fight back with words and integrity; and to Prof. Tim Tyson, who keeps me laughing and encouraged.

Of all the wonderful mentors I have been blessed with, Professors Nellie McKay and Craig Werner stand out as the most influential. I first met Nellie on a recruiting trip to the University of Wisconsin–Madison in 1998. Much to my surprise, she took time out of her hectic schedule to do lunch with me and discuss my future plans as a graduate student and scholar. Her interest in my future as a scholar was so genuine and heartfelt that I knew at once that UW was where I needed to be. Not only did she help shepherd me through the difficult obstacles of graduate school, but she also helped me to finish the program in record time and to secure a promising job. Nellie's significance in my life, however, extended far beyond her role as my academic mentor. She treated me more like a son than a former student and offered timely and critical advice to me as a junior scholar that helped bolster my spirits and career. Nellie meant the world to me and though I continue to mourn her passing, I keep her powerful legacy as scholar, teacher, activist, and mentor alive in everything that I do in and beyond the ivory tower.

Craig is a real, true-to-life genius and the most generous teacher that I have ever met. To know Craig is to love and admire him. He was chiefly responsible for helping me to develop and refine the ideas that culminate in this book. He also helped me to demystify the daunting challenges of the publishing world. Words cannot adequately express the amount of respect I have for this man, not just as a mentor, but also as a role model father, husband, and friend. While everyone else was voicing doubts about my goal to complete my doctorate in four years, Craig was encouraging me to go for it and mapping out strategies for me to succeed. To this day, I continue to rely heavily on his wisdom and guidance in helping me to stake out my own path in academe. He believed in me from the start and I owe him a debt of gratitude that I am sure I can never fully repay.

There are several friends and colleagues that have knowingly and unknowingly aided me in drafting this book. I extend deep appreciation to my dissertation group, Gretchen and Laura; to the UW crew, Dave, Greg, Lisa, Rhea, Lynn, Kim, Cherene, Amaud, Thandeka, Adrienne, and Michele. I also want to recognize the encouragement and guidance of Calvin Hall, LaMonda Horton-Stallings, Stanley James, Michael Keene, Laura Howes, Janet Atwill, Mark Anthony Neale, Herman Beavers, Michael Awkward, Michael Barnard-Donals, and Frances Smith Foster.

Special thanks go to La Vinia Delois Jennings and Chuck Maland for their generosity in reading multiple drafts of this manuscript. I also want to thank Candis LaPrade and John Easterly at LSU Press for being such wonderful and supportive editors.

Important to mention as well are the financial contributions of the College of Arts and Sciences and the Better English Fund at the University of Tennessee–Knoxville. The research leave that these funding sources provided was crucial to the completion of this project.

Finally, I thank my incredibly insightful, brilliant, and stunningly beautiful wife RaMonda. You are the love of my life, my shelter in the time of storm, and the brains behind the operation. Life has thrown us many wicked curve balls, but we have continued to swing for the fence. Thanks for hanging in there with me and always having my back. To my precocious and wickedly silly son, Elijah, I say thanks for loving daddy. You will never know how much your crazy toddler antics and warm hugs and kisses helped ease daddy's burden through some really tough times. To my beautiful new daughter, Octavia, I say thanks for restoring my belief in miracles. You are the best Christmas present I have ever received.

BREAKING THE SILENCE

INTRODUCTION

ONE OF THE MOST provocative scenes in Richard Wright's *Native Son* (1940) occurs when Buckley, the state's prosecuting attorney for Bigger Thomas's murder trial, presents Bessie Mears's mangled black corpse to the jury to reinforce his claim that Bigger raped and intentionally murdered Mary Dalton. Though often perplexed about the economic and political workings of white society, Bigger is fully aware that Buckley uses Bessie's corpse as material proof of his physical and sexual violation against Mary's white body. He observes astutely that the prosecutor was "using his having killed Bessie to kill him for his having killed Mary. . . . Though he had killed a black girl and a white girl, he knew that it would be for the death of the white girl that he would be punished. The black girl was merely 'evidence'" (383).

Even as Bigger comprehends the complex ways that Buckley and whites exploit Bessie's body, he fails to recognize his own complicity in her oppression. Consider, for example, the way that Bigger imagines Bessie's response to the exploitation of her body: "He knew that Bessie . . . though dead, though killed by him, would resent her body being used in this way. Anger quickened in him: an old feeling that Bessie often described to him when she had come from long hours of hot toil in the white folks' kitchens, a feeling of being forever commanded by others so much that thinking and feeling for one's self was impossible" (383). Emphasizing how whites mistreated Bessie during her life, Bigger implies that the exploitation of her corpse would be more offensive to her than being murdered by him. The comparison demonstrates how the discourse of black suffering allows black men to appropriate issues of gender to support their patriarchal perspectives on black women and victimization. Bigger effectively erases his own participation in Bessie's suffering by invoking white male exploitation of his victim, implying that whites are the master agents of oppression. Bessie's suffering as a black woman is never truly at issue. She merely serves as a cipher for Bigger to channel his own feelings of social emasculation. He highlights her suffering only to reinforce his indictment against whites for emasculating black men. Blind to the patriarchal power he wields over Bessie, he interprets her murder from the standpoint of a powerless victim of white oppression. Blaming whites absolves him of culpability in Bessie's death and allows him to engage the unique racial-gender victimization that she experienced at the hands of whites without having to confront his patriarchal dominance over her.

The problems of Bigger's victim status in *Native Son* have not escaped the attention of black feminist and womanist critics, most of whom believe that Wright shares his character's blindness. Literary scholars Trudier Harris and Sherley Anne Williams were the first to address Bigger's evasions and Wright's problematic representation of Bessie and other black women in *Native Son*. In her essay "Native Sons and Foreign Daughters," Harris argues that Wright's portrayal of black women as emasculators, religious fanatics, and sexual deviants encourages the reader to empathize with, rather than condemn, Bigger's cruel and, at times, violent behavior toward them. Addressing Wright's dismissive treatment of Bessie's death, Harris notes that, by portraying Bessie as a "simpering" and "weepy" character, "Wright directs our sympathies so that her death does not evoke the outrage that might be anticipated in reaction to such graphic brutality. He creates a situation in which the horrible murder of Bessie, despicable though it may be, does not strike at our emotional core as does Mary's" (79). In "Papa Dick and Sister-Woman: Reflections on Women in the Fiction of Richard Wright," Williams takes a similar position in regard to Wright's treatment of black women. Though she credits *Native Son* with opening up new avenues of exploration into issues of black rage, she criticizes Wright for denigrating black women for the sake of "glorifying the symbolic white woman." According to Williams, Wright suggests that "racism is a crime against the black man's sexual expression rather than an economic, political, and psychological crime against black people" (397). These failings, Williams concludes, severely handicap Wright's political argument in the novel, reducing black women to co-conspirators with whites in the oppression of black men.

In raising these issues, Harris and Williams confront deeply established gender patterns in African American culture. Whether their critique of Wright is definitive is not at issue here. Their fundamental premise is unquestionably true. Historically, black women have had to shoulder the burden of addressing the problems of black patriarchy, often incurring the disdain and wrath of blacks—male and female—who believe that airing such intraracial grievances against black men is detrimental to racial solidarity. In the academy, the struggle has been much the same. The burden of initiating discussions of intraracial gender issues in texts by black males has fallen primarily on black feminist critics, making them a focal point of hostility within the academy and among black men. Stanley Crouch's biting review of Toni Morrison's *Beloved* (1987) illuminates the dynamics of this intraracial resistance. He argues that *Beloved* typifies the anti-male political climate created by black women's fiction in the 1980s. The purpose of these novels, Crouch suggests, was to elevate black women to the status of the most victimized, a project that required usurping that position from black men. To accomplish this goal, black women corroborated white stereotypes of black men as wife beaters, rapists, deadbeat fathers, and child molesters, clearing the path for their own social recognition. Crouch insists that *Beloved* exemplifies this trend and was designed "to placate sentimental feminist ideology, and to make sure that the vision of [the] black woman as the most scorned and rebuked of the victims doesn't weaken" (40). Condemning black women as collaborators with whites in black male social emasculation, Crouch claims that black women authors address the oppression of black women as a ploy to generate political and cultural sympathy. The social cost of this sympathy, he insists, is the further debasement of the already disenfranchised black male.

This type of attack obviously seeks to discredit black feminist claims against black men as spiteful and perverse. But it also seeks to silence black women who fear being labeled emasculators or race traitors. What becomes clear is that victim status allows Crouch and black men to scapegoat black women and ignore suffering under patriarchy. Witness how Crouch presents Ernest Gaines and Charles Johnson as examples of black writers that avoid the "reductive" representations of oppression that plague *Beloved*. "Had Morrison higher intentions when she appropriated the conventions of a holocaust tale, *Beloved* might stand next to, or outdistance, Ernest Gaines's *The Autobiography of Miss Jane Pittman* (1971) and Charles Johnson's *Oxherding Tale* (1982), neither of which submits to the contrived, post-Baldwin vision" that social persecution can build moral character and heighten political insight (43). To take nothing away from Gaines's and Johnson's fine novels, Crouch's comparison implies that black male authors are better suited to address black female suffering than black women, a claim which epitomizes the problems and dangers of black male victim status.

My chief aim in *Breaking the Silence* is to expose and explode the victim status upon which black patriarchy is premised. To do so, I examine how the social and cultural politics of slavery, white male domination, and female oppression (black and white) inform—and at times distort—black men's perceptions of themselves as victimizers of black women. These perceptions problematize black men's social and political responses to women (black and white) and to each other and make it difficult to imagine productive paths beyond the social and cultural impasse of black males' victim mind-set. The situation is further complicated by the fact that black patriarchy is partly sustained by unintentional black female complicity. Few black women openly reject patriarchy, in part because black women's self-sacrifice is widely celebrated in the black community. Women who prioritize the needs/wants of their men and families over their own receive cultural compensation in social displays of gratitude, admiration, and respect. The cultural affirmation of self-sacrifice compels black women to ignore suffering under patriarchy to support black men and preserve cultural solidarity, thereby rendering black women accomplices in their own subjugation.

To date, black male critics have paid disturbingly little attention to the interlocking gender and cultural dynamics of black patriarchy. My study directly addresses this crucial oversight by complicating the static victimized/victimizer, oppressor/oppressed binaries implicit in many discussions of black oppression. Complicating these binaries allows for more complex examinations of disparities in power and social agency across racial and gender differences. Even those who have suffered themselves can become "surrogate" oppressors. All too often, victimized appeals to social "innocence" and "blamelessness" erase social agency (for black women and men) and reify white oppression.

A brief overview of how key black-male-authored texts—spanning from slavery to the Black Arts Movement—have treated black female suffering underscores how these victimized appeals have historically functioned to distort black men's notions of manhood and resistance. In *Narrative of the Life of Frederick Douglass, An American Slave, Written by Himself* (1845), one of the most significant black-male-authored texts of the nineteenth century, Douglass strategically uses black female suffering to illuminate the horrors of slavery for his mostly northern white readership. Douglass portrays black women, such as his Aunt Hester, as powerless and weak in order to dramatize the manifold ways that whites exploit and mistreat them. In *Witnessing Slavery* (1979) Frances Smith Foster argues that his monolithic portraits of black women as "utter victims" elide the resolve and strength of the many slave women who fought against the system of slavery as tenaciously as their male counterparts. Rather than provide a realistic representation of the experience of slavery for black women, Douglass views black female suffering as a part of black men's emasculation. I would add to Foster's insightful observations that these portraits also reveal black male anxiety of being "feminized" by slavery. This dynamic is brought into focus when Douglass foregrounds Aunt Hester's brutal beating by her slave owner/rapist, Captain Anthony, for disobeying his command to stay away from a male slave on a nearby plantation. The thinly veiled sexual references in the scene clearly cast the beating as a figurative rape. After stripping Hester "from neck to waist," Captain Anthony "made her get upon . . . [a] stool, and tied her hands to . . . [a] hook." He adds, "She now stood fair for his infernal purpose" (6). Douglass's emphasis, however, is not on Hester's experience of suffering as a black woman, but on the emotional trauma he experiences as a child having to witness the beating/rape: "I was so terrified and horror-stricken at the *sight*, that I hid myself in a closet, and dared not venture out till long after the bloody transaction was over. I expected it would be my turn next" (7; my italics). Douglass's fear of being next in line to receive a beating can be read as his anxiety as a black man about being symbolically raped and feminized by his white masters. The fear of rape and feminization is prevalent throughout the narrative and explains why for Douglass acquiring freedom is inextricably bound up with acquiring manhood. While Douglass's heroism has been rightly celebrated, few critics have perceived that this link between freedom and manhood damages black women by ensconcing their social agency within a gendered discourse of black male resistance, fostering the idea that black liberation is dependent upon black men acquiring manhood.

In Charles Chesnutt's turn-of-the-century novel *The Marrow of Tradition* (1901), black women again function as symbolic ciphers in the author's exploration of black manhood and resistance. Specifically, the novel focuses on the political debates over black resistance that emerge between racial idealist Dr. William Miller and militant black nationalist Josh Green. These debates function thematically to contextualize Chesnutt's racial politics, illuminating that either racial idealism or black nationalism taken to the extreme can exacerbate the social and political problems of the black community. Chesnutt's failure to include a black woman in these debates exposes his gendered blind spot, a blind spot that is most noticeable in his stereotypical portraits of Mammy Jane and Miller's wife Janet, the only significant black female characters in the novel. Representing all that is problematic about white accommodationism, Mammy Jane is an Aunt Jemima figure who treats her white employers with godlike deference and holds contempt for blacks that challenge the status quo. In stark contrast, Janet is a beautiful, well-educated, morally upright, near-white mulatto who represents the ideal black wife and mother. The narrator underscores Janet's "exceptional" qualities with a telling and ironic declaration that she is so refined in appearance and manner that she is often mistaken in public for her white half-sister Mrs. Carteret, who lived in town. That Chesnutt creates such stereotypical images of black women is quite revealing, especially given how he complicates the "angry black man" stereotype in his rendering of Josh Green to illustrate his humanity and the legitimacy of his anger toward whites. Refusing, consciously and unconsciously, to extend the same complexity to his black female characters, Chesnutt bankrupts them of their individuality, reducing them to thematic props to advance his notions of black womanhood and his masculinist approach to black resistance.

Chesnutt's rendering of Janet in the closing scenes of the novel brings the problems of his perspective dramatically into focus. He uses her to initiate Miller's assertion of manhood and to establish him as a heroic figure who is both militant and moral. His political agenda becomes clear in the way that Janet serves as the catalyst for Miller's daring and courageous stance against Mr. Carteret, a powerful white supremacist who helps orchestrate a race riot. In this crucial scene Janet functions as Miller's primary motivation for rebuking Carteret's white supremacy and refusing to provide medical assistance to his dying son. Outraged by his wife's suffering over the loss of their child to racial violence, Miller vows to stay by her side and protect her against white lynch mobs. He tells Carteret, whom he forces to appear in person to request medical assistance, "[I]t is not safe to leave [Janet] unattended. My duty calls me here, by the side of my dead child and my suffering wife! I cannot go with you. There is a just God in heaven! —as you have sown, so may you reap!" (320). Miller emerges as a heroic figure because he embraces his manly duties as his wife's protector and avenges his son's death by refusing medical treatment to Carteret's son. Chesnutt confirms Miller's hero status in Carteret's internal reflections: "[H]e could not blame the doctor for his stand. He was indeed conscious of a certain involuntary admiration for a man who held in his hands the power of life and death, and could use it, with strict justice, to avenge his own wrongs" (321). By having Carteret respond to Miller with respect and admiration, Chesnutt conveys that black men can assert power and authority over their white male counterparts despite their subordinate social and political status. The problem is that Chesnutt confirms Miller's masculinity by portraying Janet as a helpless victim deserving of justice and in desperate need of protection. Her experiences of suffering and empowerment are never under consideration. She functions as a cipher, like Bessie in Wright's *Native Son*, to convey the experiences of racial oppression for black men. Thus her actions direct the reader's attention to Miller's circumstances as a black man and reveal little about her experiences of oppression as a black woman.

A similar dynamic is at work in the final scene of the novel. Janet provides the opportunity for Miller to assist the Carteret baby and emerge as a heroic moral figure without compromising his militancy. Chesnutt orchestrates the scene so that Miller becomes softened by Mrs. Carteret's desperate pleas for mercy and agrees to let Janet decide his course of action. This literary maneuver is critical because it positions Janet as the catalyst for reversing Miller's original decision to deny medical care. When she ultimately decides to aid her half-sister, Miller appears noble rather than weak for helping the Carterets because he clearly acts out of love for his wife and not to please or impress whites. Even though Chesnutt elevates Janet above Mrs. Carteret and white women in terms of morality and virtue—she does not lie, cheat, or steal like her white counterparts—he bankrupts her of complexity and agency. Her selfless act of clemency is radically in line with the ideal of Victorian white womanhood she embodies. What Janet's portrait reveals is that Chesnutt cannot conceptualize a redeeming version of black womanhood beyond a problematic white ideal.

In his Harlem Renaissance novel *Home to Harlem* (1928), Claude McKay employs primitivistic, rather than genteel, notions of black female sexuality to examine the complexity of black manhood. He portrays black women as hypersexual, aggressive, vindictive, and violent beings whose primary desire is to control and manipulate black men. In most cases these women are so desperate for male companionship that they resort to extreme measures to attract mates, often providing men with financial assistance in exchange for their sexual loyalty. When these relationships fall apart—usually due to the male partner's infidelity—the result is often violence on the part of the duped women who, in most cases, attack their female competitors rather than the unfaithful men. These primitivistic notions of black female sexuality debilitate black women by erasing their humanity and distorting the social, economic, and cultural variables that shape their lives. In the black community these distortions fortify the destructive patriarchal thinking that justifies abuse of black women. McKay's treatment of domestic violence in the relationship between Jake, the central protagonist, and his girlfriend Rose illuminates this intraracial dynamic. When, in a fit of rage, Jake gives Rose "two savage slaps full in her face" for calling him a "poor black stiff," McKay encourages the reader to empathize with Jake rather than Rose, whom he characterizes as a sadomasochist that views physical abuse as a sign of affection and manhood. In the aftermath of the fight Jake agonizes over his actions, while Rose brags to one of her friends. Failing to address the patriarchal conditioning that engenders Rose's sadomasochism, McKay leaves the reader to accept Jake's self-righteous and gendered claim that Rose "jest made me do it" (116). Rose, the true victim of domestic violence, becomes responsible for her own victimization.

Though certainly more subtle, Ralph Ellison's post–World War II novel *Invisible Man* (1952) enacts a disturbingly similar kind of gendered displacement. The most significant instance occurs when Trueblood, a poor black sharecropper, impregnates his teenage daughter Matty Lou and blames his incestuous act on a dream about sexual conquest of a white woman. In *Inspiriting Influences* (1989), Michael Awkward challenges Houston Baker's conceptualization of Trueblood's incest as culturally redeeming, arguing that Trueblood's dream in fact functions to erase the experience of rape for Matty Lou. Awkward observes that Trueblood's "dream of sexual conquest with a white woman while in the home of an affluent white man necessarily brings to mind images of lynching and castration of Afro-American males by white men because of the threat of black male sexuality. Consequently, Trueblood's actual presence inside his daughter assumes less importance in the text than his dream encounter with an unnamed white woman" (86). This act of black female erasure is further bolstered, Awkward argues, by Ellison's omission of Matty Lou's perspective on the event. That Ellison chooses to disregard Matty Lou's version is especially significant in light of the salient way he emphasizes oppression of white women. In the "Battle Royal" scene, for example, Ellison highlights the social oppression of the naked, blond dancer who is nearly mobbed by a drove of intoxicated white men after they parade her in front of a terrified group of black teenage boys. The narrator observes, "They caught her just as she reached a door, raised her from the floor, and tossed her as college boys are tossed at a hazing, and above her red, fixed-smiling lips I saw the terror and disgust in her eyes, almost like my own terror and that which I saw in some of the other boys" (20). Ellison and the Invisible Man recognize the terror and disgust behind the white woman's "fixed-smiling lips," demonstrating their awareness that white women, like black men, must don social masks as a means of social and economic survival. Ellison's failure to extend a similar consideration to black women underscores the pattern of black men's disregard for black female resistance and suffering.

· During the Black Arts Movement in the 1960s and 1970s the cultural disregard for black women grew even more pronounced, as illustrated by Amiri Baraka's *Dutchman* (1964). Presenting black men as the chief victims of white oppression, the play addresses the underlying social and psychological politics of black assimilation. Baraka explores these complex issues by showing how white seductress Lula, symbolizing the white establishment, cajoles Clay, a symbol of the black middle class, into expressing his hatred of whites, which leads directly to his murder. Clay's expression of rage is culturally empowering, allowing him to identify the social forces that emasculate him. Baraka shows, however, that his empowerment comes at a high cost; Lula kills Clay when she learns of his repressed feelings about whites. The problem is that Baraka and *Dutchman* characterize black oppression as a dilemma of emasculation for black men. The result is that black women's experiences of suffering get erased. This dynamic is dramatically displayed in Clay's brief references to blues and jazz singer Bessie Smith in his heated exchange with Lula. Clay invokes Smith—the only black female presence in the play—to expose white liberalism as corrupt and to promote black violence as the most effective strategy to combat white oppression. Illuminating his bitterness toward liberal-minded whites, like Lula, who claim to understand black male suffering, Clay rants, "Old bald-headed four-eyed ofays popping their fingers . . . and don't know yet what they're doing. They say, 'I love Bessie Smith.' And don't even understand that Bessie Smith is saying, 'Kiss my ass, kiss my black unruly ass.' Before love, suffering, desire, anything you can explain, she's saying, and very plainly, 'Kiss my black ass.' And if you don't know that, it's you that's doing the kissing" (34).

Clay and Baraka present Bessie Smith as a trickster figure that masks her hatred of whites in her singing. Under scrutiny here is the idea that sympathetic whites can identify with black male suffering through intimate cultural or physical contact (read: white heterosexual intercourse with black men). When Clay asserts that Smith harbors angst toward whites which they can neither recognize nor comprehend because of deep-seated white supremacy, his aim is not to illuminate black women's rage or political subversiveness toward whites. Rather, he wants to expose the insidious paternalism of whites that claim to comprehend black men's social and racial realities. This explains why he condemns rather than champions Smith's subversive strategy after he uses her as an example to illustrate white blindness to black rage. He and Baraka view Smith and blacks that disguise their hatred of whites in any form as politically weak and ineffective: "If Bessie Smith had killed some white people she wouldn't have needed that music. She could have talked very straight and plain about the world. No metaphors. No grunts. No wiggles in the dark of her soul. Just straight two and two are four" (35). Smith is not a true revolutionary, then, because she is not "manly" enough to express her feelings openly and strike down her oppressors. That the only black woman mentioned in the play is ultimately characterized as counterproductive to black empowerment is very telling. What becomes clear is that Clay and Baraka cannot conceptualize the possibility of black women combating white oppression on their own terms.

It should be noted that Baraka no longer identifies himself as a revolutionary black nationalist or openly defends the patriarchal and abusive mind-set that was the hallmark of the Black Arts Movement. His famous essay "The Myth of 'Negro Literature'" (1966), written during the heyday of his black nationalist thinking, provides insights into his previous mind-set and explains why black women do not receive serious consideration in *Dutchman*. He writes that if black writers want to tap into the "legitimate [African American] cultural tradition" they need to "utilize the entire spectrum of the American experience from the point of view of the emotional history of the black man in this country: as its victim and its chronicler" (111–12). Treating the oppression of black men as representative of all black people, Baraka reinforces the idea that black men's experiences of oppression are normative. In perpetuating this idea, he also reestablishes cultural taboos that discourage black women from speaking out about their gender oppression, especially as it relates to black men. To this end, Baraka ironically reproduces the assimilationist mind-set that his play ostensibly repudiates, forcing black women into a cultural double-bind: either they can remain silent and internalize their experiences of abuse and mistreatment, or they can vocalize their frustration and anger at the risk of being culturally ostracized.

Black women scholars, writers, and activists started the black feminist movement in the 1970s to address these patterns of silencing and erasure within and beyond the black literary field. Frustrated with the exclusionary politics of black liberation movements (i.e., civil rights, black power, and black studies) that treated all blacks as male and the mainstream feminist movement that treated all women as white, they developed a black feminist perspective to account for their unique experiences of oppression and empowerment as black women and to critique dominant and reactionary discourses that ignored their concerns. A top priority of black feminist scholars was to establish academic credibility for black feminism. To do so, they had to address several difficult questions: What are the distinguishing characteristics of black feminist methodology? What constitutes a black feminist critique? And, who is eligible to perform black feminist criticism? The genealogy of debate can be traced through key texts by Barbara Smith, Deborah E. McDowell, Hazel Carby, and Michael Awkward. While other critics have made significant contributions to black feminism, the four writers discussed here are universally recognized for their insights and influence on the development of the discourse. It should be noted that these writers have revised and reworked aspects of their germinal essays and engaged many of the problems I outline below in their subsequent writings. My purpose in mapping out the intellectual trajectory of black feminism is to show the evolution of black *male* feminism and to engage the origins of the critical debates that shape this study. Premised as it was on a radically raced and classed perspective, mainstream (white) U.S. feminist theory was not immediately useful to me in the early stages of my intellectual development as a black male feminist. In this introduction I speak more generally about the politics of exclusion within mainstream feminism and how those politics ignited the black feminist movement within academe. I do not give these issues a full airing because they have been widely and productively engaged by Elliott Butler-Evans, Barbara Christian, Thadious Davis, Frances Smith Foster, Trudier Harris, June Jordan, Deborah E. McDowell, Nellie McKay, Barbara Smith, Valerie Smith, Hortense Spillers, Claudia Tate, Alice Walker, Cheryl Wall, Michelle Wallace, Mary Helen Washington, and, more recently, by bell hooks, Michael Awkward, Devon Carbado, Patricia Hill-Collins, Mark Anthony Neale, and Kimberle Williams Crenshaw.

In her groundbreaking essay "Toward a Black Feminist Criticism" (1977), Barbara Smith introduced the dominant theme of black feminist criticism and the central premise of this book: the idea that race, gender, and class are interlocking factors that inform the complex reality of black women's oppression. Her idea was particularly important because it exposed the political limitations of white feminist and black-male-centered approaches to literature. Specifically, she showed how white feminists frequently obscured their racial privilege by focusing on gender oppression and, similarly, how black male critics obscured their gender privilege by focusing on racial oppression.

Smith's formulation of a black feminist approach to literature was not without its own problems, however. She insisted, for instance, that only black women and black lesbians could adequately engage with black women's writing because, unlike whites and black men, they were not invested in dominant racial and gender regimes. Moreover, she asserted that black women shared a common language and experience of oppression which could be used to distinguish black women's writing from that of whites and black men. Relying on an essentialist notion of black womanhood,

Smith unintentionally repeats a pattern of stereotyping that she condemns in criticism by whites and black men. Viewing black women's experiences of oppression and struggle as monolithic, Smith failed to account for political, social, and cultural diversity among black women.

An important footnote to Smith's perspective here is that in 1977 when her essay appeared, she collaborated with members of the Combahee River Collective, Demita Frazier and Beverly Smith, to write the landmark black feminist manifesto "A Black Feminist Statement," a text that ultimately refutes the notion that men because of their biological maleness are inherently sexist and uneducable: "We have a great deal of criticism and loathing for what men have been socialized to be in this society: what they support, how they act, and how they oppress. But we do not have the misguided notion that it is their maleness, per se—i.e., their biological maleness—that makes them what they are. As Black women we find any type of biological determinism a particularly dangerous and reactionary basis upon which to build a politic" (17). That "A Black Feminist Statement" and Smith's "Toward a Black Feminist Criticism" were produced in roughly the same year is very telling. It reflects the complicated trajectory of Smith's development as an activist and scholar. More importantly, it shows that she was aware, on some level, of the potential problems of biological essentialism in the earliest stages of her career.

In her essay "New Directions for Black Feminist Criticism" (1980), Deborah E. McDowell addresses the ideological pitfalls of Smith's methodology in "Toward a Black Feminist Criticism" by posing a series of probing questions about her representation of black women's experiences. McDowell asks, "[I]s there a monolithic Black female language? Do Black female high school dropouts, welfare mothers, college graduates, and Ph.D.s share a common language? Are there regional variations in this common language? . . . Are there noticeable differences between the languages of Black females and Black males?" (154). Though McDowell poses these questions to illuminate the vagueness of

Smith's definition of black female language, she never attempts to answer them herself. Nor does she abandon the basic premise of Smith's argument, that black women share a distinct language and set of cultural experiences. Rather she poses these questions to underscore the importance of clearly defining what constitutes a black feminist methodology. Her fear is that without such clarity black feminism will never "move beyond mere critical jargon" (154), undermining its usefulness for engaging black women's literature and addressing the problems it identifies.

McDowell's most significant departure from Smith concerns her attitude toward male and Western modes of criticism, particularly in regard to the question of who can engage in black feminist criticism. Unlike Smith, McDowell recognizes the problem of rejecting all modes of criticism that have not been established by black women. Though she is aware of the difficulties, she feels that men, black or white, can practice black feminism. Ultimately, she insists that critical perspective rather than gender is the most significant gauge of legitimacy: "I agree with Annette Kolodny that feminist criticism would be 'shortsighted if it summarily rejected all the inherited tools of critical analysis simply because they are male and western.' We should, rather, salvage what we find useful in past methodologies, reject what we do not, and, where necessary, move toward 'inventing new methods of analysis'" (156). While McDowell significantly broadens Smith's definition of who has access to black feminism to include participation by whites and black men, she rehearses Smith's essentialist representation of black women. She argues, for instance, that black feminist criticism could apply to "any criticism written by a Black woman regardless of her subject or perspective—a book written by a male from a feminist or political perspective, a book written by a Black woman or about Black women authors in general, or any writings by women" (155). Her definition of what constitutes a black feminist criticism uncritically privileges black female perspectives, reproducing problems similar to those plaguing Smith's representation. Rather than clarifying the question of what constitutes a black feminist methodology, McDowell's portrait of black women only invokes more uncertainty.

In *Reconstructing Womanhood: The Emergence of the Afro-American Woman Novelist* (1987), Hazel Carby challenges the essentialist tendencies of black feminism, treating the emergent discourse as a problem rather than a solution to black female erasure in the academy. Her chief criticism of black feminism is that it shares unacknowledged motivations with other reactionary discourses—namely, to legitimate itself within a "framework of bourgeois humanistic discourse" (15). The desire for intellectual legitimacy, she argues, has prompted black feminists to focus their energies on trying to "discover, prove, and legitimate the intellectual worthiness of black women" as a path to claiming "their rightful placement as both subjects and creators of the curriculum" (16). Carby asserts that by preoccupying themselves with intellectual legitimacy, black women accept rather than challenge the "prevailing paradigms pre-dominant in the academy" (15). She is also critical of black feminism because it "has too frequently been reduced to an experimental relationship that exists between black women as critics and black women as writers who represent black women's reality" (16). This reliance on a shared experience has, in turn, produced an ahistorical theoretical framework with essentialist tendencies. Black feminism "presupposes the existence of a tradition" of black women's literature and then "concentrat[es] on establishing a narrative of that tradition" informed by its essentialist views. Seeking to avoid patterns of essentialism, Carby does not "assume the existence of a tradition or traditions of black writing" and flatly rejects the idea that there is such a thing as a distinctive black female language. She insists that "no language or experience is divorced from the shared context in which different groups that share language express their differing group interests" (16–17). Rather, "language is accented differently by competing groups, and therefore the terrain of language is a terrain of power relations. The struggle within language reveals the nature of the structure of social relations and the hierarchy of power, not the nature of one particular group." Given the relational dynamics of power and language, "black and feminist cannot be absolute, transhistorical forms (or form) of identity" (17).

Though Carby objects to the label "black feminist," her political and ideological concerns are similar to Smith's and McDowell's. The focus of Carby's project, for instance, is to examine the myriad complexities of black female erasure in white women's writing to expose how white women activists and feminists have historically used appeals to "sisterhood" to obscure the ways that race has shaped their politics of resistance and struggle. She exposes these patterns of elision by emphasizing the intersection of race, class, and gender in the construction of white and black women's identities. Such an emphasis, Carby argues, will provide a necessary revision to feminist historiography, demonstrating that white women were "not only the subjects but also the perpetrators of oppression" (18). Despite her reservations concerning black feminist practice, Carby shares Smith's belief that race, gender, and class are interlocking factors that must be considered when addressing black women's realities. The most significant difference in Carby's appropriation of this idea is that she extends it to include examinations of white women's identity, observing that race "as a central category does not necessarily need to be about black women" (18). The assertion that race is a crucial component of white women's identity does not lie outside the scope of black feminism. Rather, it underscores the importance of making full use of the opportunities provided by race-conscious and class-conscious models.

I am acutely aware that black female critics developed a black feminist methodology in part to address the problematic ways in which black male critics approached black female texts. Like black male novelists, black male critics too often focus on what they perceive as the negative representation of black men by black female authors. The evasion of the issues raised in black women's literature convinced many black feminists to conclude that black men were incapable of adequately reading black women's literature.

Even as it acknowledged the problems with most black male criticism, Michael Awkward's provocative essay "A Black Man's Place in Black Feminist Criticism" asserted that critical perspective, not gender, should be the gauge for determining who can practice black feminist criticism. Adapting Sherley Anne Williams's notion of "womanist theory," based in part on Alice Walker's definition of the term, he argued for the possibility of a black male feminism that interrogates black patriarchy and encourages feminist discussions of black women's texts, while maintaining as its ultimate goal the mental well-being of the entire black community. To establish a theoretical basis for black male feminism, Awkward refers to Hortense Spillers's theory in "Mama's Baby, Papa's Maybe" of the "repressed female within" the black male subject. He argues that Spillers's theory "represents a fruitful starting point for new, potentially nonpatriarchal figurations of family and of black males' relationship to the female" because rather than viewing the "black 'female' as strictly Other for the Afro-American male, Spillers's afrocentric re-visioning of psychoanalytic theory insists that we consider the 'female' as an important aspect of the repressed in the black male self" (14). To this end, her theory offers a useful and productive means by which black men and women can address issues of patriarchy because it "demands neither the erasure of the black gendered other's subjectivity . . . nor the relegation of males to prone, domestic, or other limiting or objectifiable positions" (15). Awkward insists that if black men are to be of value to the feminist project they must utilize Spillers's and Williams's insights and "provide illuminating and persuasive readings of gender as it is constituted for blacks in America and sophisticated, informed, contentious critiques of phallocentric practices in an effort to redefine our notions of black male and female textuality" (15). He further outlines the key difference between black male feminism and black feminism produced by individual black women, writing that "black male feminism must be both rigorous in engaging these texts [black women's literature] and self-reflective enough to avoid, at all costs, the types of patronizing, marginalizing gestures that have traditionally characterized Afro-American male intellectuals' response to black womanhood" (16). The crucial point here for Awkward—and for my own study—is that biological maleness is a factor that must remain under scrutiny within black male feminism because black men benefit directly and indirectly from patriarchy regardless of their political investments. To ignore the social advantages of biological maleness as black male feminists is to risk complicity in the very institution of patriarchy we strive to dismantle.

While Awkward furnishes a useful model for black male feminism, his delineations of how black men oppress and exploit black women suggest that black women are powerless and helpless victims. This monolithic portrait has the effect of bankrupting black women of any individuality and social agency. As such, it forecloses the possibilities of addressing the complex dynamics of black women's agency, on the one hand, and the relational complicity of black men and women in sustaining the system of black patriarchy on the other.

To underscore the importance of engaging complicity and black women's agency, I will refer to Awkward's critique of Toni Morrison's *Sula* (1973) to show the limitations of his reading of Eva Peace as a victim under patriarchy. In his essay Awkward references Eva's murdering of her son Plum to draw attention to black men's skewed perspective on manhood and black women. His chief aim is to show how many "black-males-in-crisis" internalize notions of black manhood premised on the erasure of black women's desires. Using Spillers's theory as a guidepost, he examines Morrison's critique of this problematic notion of black manhood through her rendering of Eva's motivations for murder. He concludes that Eva's fear is that "Plum's pitiful, infantile state has the potential to reduce *her* to a static female function of self-sacrificing mother" (20; italics in text) and thus she kills him in a radical act of self-preservation. I contend that Eva murders her son because he fails to recognize and appreciate the value of her self-sacrifice, *not* because she fears or rejects the expectation of self-sacrifice for black women. As I outline below, Eva has internalized patriarchy to the point that she attaches pride to her self-sacrificial mothering and uses it to manipulate and control her family. When Eva explains her motivation for murder to Hannah, she emphasizes her sacrifices to keep Plum alive and expresses intense frustration at his inability to make productive use of her efforts: "It was such a carryin' on to get him born and to keep him alive. Just to keep his little heart beating and his little old lungs cleared and look like when he came back from that war he wanted to get back in. After all that carryin' on, just gettin' him out and keepin' him alive, he wanted to crawl back in my womb and well . . . I ain't got the room no more even if he could do it" (71). Eva murders Plum, then, because he fails to live up to his end of the "patriarchal bargain." He does not repay her sacrifices with a celebratory life as a "man." Rather, he resorts to drugs as a coping mechanism after the war and retreats into his mother's home to receive emotional and material nurturing. His failure undermines Eva's extreme sacrifices as a mother and ultimately provokes her to kill him.

Eva's deep investment in patriarchy and self-sacrifice is reflected vividly in her heated argument with Sula several years after she murders Plum. Eva initiates the argument by invoking self-sacrifice to shame Sula into apologizing for not keeping in touch over her ten-year stint away from the Bottom. You were "quick enough [to keep in touch] when you wanted something," she chastises Sula, and then begins to relay examples of her philanthropy toward her granddaughter. Unmoved by Eva's shame tactics, Sula cuts her off abruptly, "Don't talk to me about how much you gave me, Big Mamma, and how much I owe you or none of that." Eva returns sharply, "Oh? I ain't supposed to mention it?" (92). Her sardonic tone reveals her belief—voiced earlier in the narrative to Hannah— that her children and grandchildren owe her respect and admiration for her sacrifices of motherhood. Sula does not give in to Eva's demands for an apology or express gratitude for her self-sacrifice because she rejects the patriarchal thinking upon which her grandmother's notions of womanhood are premised. What is most revealing about this heated exchange is that Eva associates Sula's rebellious attitude with her status as a single woman and suggests getting married and having children as a remedy. "It'll settle you" (92), she opines. Given Eva's disastrous marriage to BoyBoy and her excruciatingly painful experiences as a mother, it would seem that she would understand and appreciate Sula's resistance. That Eva tries instead to police Sula into repeating unsuccessful patterns of marriage and mothering reveals the extreme depth of her complicity and casts light on a major obstacle to dismantling patriarchy. She is so deeply invested in self-sacrifice that she cannot conceptualize a viable model of womanhood outside the domain of marriage and mothering. As such, she misreads Sula's desire for independence and self-discovery as signs of immaturity and selfishness. Complicity, then, blinds Eva to alternatives to self-sacrifice and renders her a gatekeeper of patriarchy.

Awkward's emphasis on addressing the problems of black patriarchy as it regards black men severely hampers his capacity to engage with Eva's black female agency. Such an engagement is important because it illuminates the complexity of her subjugation as a black woman, including the way she is unintentionally complicit in the maintenance of black patriarchy. Addressing these kinds of gender practices in relation to the problematic ways that black men conceptualize their manhood is critical, as Morrison observes in "The Official Story: Dead Man Golfing." Putting an end to patriarchy, she writes, is a far more complex task than simply "reeducat[ing] and socializ[ing] men into non-aggressive and respectful behavior" toward women (xxiii). It requires rather a more sophisticated examination of the gender, social, and political variables that sustain black patriarchy, including those unintentionally perpetuated by its victims. Ultimately, if black male feminism is to help overturn black patriarchy, it must widen the scope of its critical inquiry across gender lines.

Even as a chief aim of *Breaking the Silence* is to challenge overdetermined and oversimplified representations of black men's experience of oppression, privilege, and resistance, I will still make use of the terms *black patriarchy* and *white supremacy*. While it is certainly true that these terms have been used in reductive ways that belie the complexity of the cultural phenomena that they represent, they remain useful if utilized with "caution and qualifications," as Ania Loomba observes in her insightful study *Colonialism/ Postcolonialism*. Regarding the use of the term *patriarchy* in feminist criticism, Loomba argues astutely that the term is

> applicable to the extent that it indicates male domination over women. But the ideology and practices of male domination are historically, geographically and culturally variable. English patriarchal structures were different in the sixteenth century from what they are today, and they varied also between classes, then and now. All of these are further distinct from patriarchy in China, which is also variable over time and social groupings. But of course all of these also have something in common, so feminist theory has had to weave between analyzing the universals and the particulars in the oppression. Patriarchy then becomes a useful shorthand for conveying a structure of inequity, which is, in practice, highly variable because it always works alongside other social structures. (18)

It is this strategic weaving "between analyzing the universals and the particulars in the oppression" that most aptly describes my use of the terms *black patriarchy* and *white supremacy*. Certainly, the most formidable challenge is to avoid reproducing the very problematic cultural constructs that one ostensibly seeks to identify and critique.

Breaking the Silence represents my effort to break the cultural silence regarding black complicity in oppression that allows patriarchy to thrive in the black community. To accomplish this task, I perform close readings of key African American texts in each chapter and use them as models for understanding and resolving the complex and varied forms of complicity. My aim is to demonstrate the potential for using literature to develop viable strategies that can disrupt complicity and explode patriarchy.

Chapter 1, "Love Jones: A Black Male Feminist Critique of Chester Himes's *If He Hollers Let Him Go*," investigates the crisis of black male identity that prompts Himes and his central protagonist, Bob Jones, to perceive women (black and white) as proponents of black male social emasculation. Focusing attention on the marginalized perspectives of the black women in the text, this chapter reconsiders the received image of Bob Jones as a "Black Everyman." Illuminating Himes's phallocentric assumptions regarding black women, this perspective calls attention to the erasure of the black female social perspectives in the novel. To redress this erasure, I consider Ella Mae's criticism of Bob Jones's relationship with Madge, and her compelling critique of his black masculine crisis. Such consideration sheds new light on the gendered politics of Jones's perspective. It becomes evident, for example, that Jones's understanding of his socioeconomic oppression is linked to his frustration at not being able to fully dominate women sexually. Presenting but not fully comprehending these contradictions, Himes's project of black resistance to white racism is gendered in ways that reinforce rather than subvert white patriarchy.

Chapter 2, "Black Patriarchy and the Dilemma of Black Women's Complicity in James Baldwin's *Go Tell It on the Mountain*," situates Baldwin as an important literary practitioner of black male feminism. It also shows how *Go Tell It* functions as a corrective text to *If He Hollers*, accounting for the cultural victim status that allows black men to oppress black women with impunity. In *Go Tell It* Gabriel never comes to grips with his abusive behavior toward women because he believes that, as a man and the chief target of social persecution, he is entitled to black women's unwavering loyalty and servitude. Exploding the victim mentality of black men is difficult, Baldwin demonstrates, because black women rely heavily on the male-focused black community for support and thus tend to accept rather than challenge patriarchal thinking. This deep reliance on a male-focused community explains why even Florence—the only woman in *Go Tell It* who openly defies male authority and rejects self-sacrifice—has difficulty severing ties with a black church that caters to black men. Doing so will alienate her culturally and require that she suffer her life-threatening cancer (read: patriarchal resistance) alone. Baldwin's rendering of Florence demonstrates the dangers of political and cultural isolation. Even though she is equipped with important knowledge about patriarchy, Florence still needs a community from which to draw strength and support. Without such a community she cannot validate her experiences or successfully navigate the cultural pressures to embrace patriarchy.

Chapter 3, "'Killing the White Girl First': Understanding the Politics of Black Manhood in Toni Morrison's *Paradise*," explores the gender-informed cultural variables that produce and sustain the destructive patriarchal mind-set discussed in chapter 1. Through an investigation of how the men of Ruby justify their killing of the "white" woman in the convent as an act of resistance to white male domination, I reveal how the discourse of black (coded male) suffering distorts black men's notions of victimization. Moreover, I show how this discourse of suffering silences the black women in Ruby, making them unintentionally complicit in their own subjugation. Highlighting the complexity of this complicity illustrates the difficulty of dismantling black patriarchy. It also underscores the importance of gender revision for black men and women.

Chapter 4, "'So Much of What We Know Ain't So': The Other Gender in Toni Cade Bambara's *The Salt Eaters*," probes the historical and cultural roots of the "strong black woman" model of black womanhood to demonstrate how self-sacrifice and cultural sacrifice hamper black female empowerment and create an unhealthy social crutch for black men. By examining the contentious relationship that Velma, the central protagonist, has with her sister Palma and her godmother Sophie Heywood, I illustrate the ways that Velma unintentionally reinforces the patriarchal regimes that she ostensibly repudiates, becoming a policing agent for black female self-sacrifice. Foregrounding this problematic aspect of Velma's ideology brings the gender-race crisis of her husband

James and bus driver Fred Holt into focus. Both internalize black male victim status and expectations of black women's self-sacrifice, making it difficult for them to come to grips with their victimizing patterns as black men and to comprehend black women who reject traditional nurturing roles.

In chapter 5 I use Walter Mosley's resistance framework in his essay "Giving Back" to ground my investigation into the black male feminist politics of his collection of stories *Always Outnumbered, Always Outgunned* (1998) and his novel *Walkin' the Dog* (1999). Illuminating the cultural source and complexity of black complicity, this framework calls attention to how intraracial gender and cultural politics handicap black male resistance efforts, particularly in poor, urban centers. Examining the mentorship between the central protagonist Socrates and his unofficially adopted son Darryl in *Always Outnumbered*, the first half of the chapter considers the ways that black male rage and anger is systematically turned against other black men. This focus casts light on the ways that black men are unintentionally complicit in their own oppression. Highlighting this complicity draws attention to patterns of black-on-black male violence that inadvertently reify the status quo. The second half of the chapter focuses on *Walkin' the Dog* and engages the story of the slave rebellion that Socrates relays to his black discussion group to outline the problematic notions of black male resistance that frustrate black self-determination and awareness of complicity. Socrates's story calls conventional victimizer/victimized binaries into question, revealing as it does so how the legacy of black violence against whites and each other corrupts contemporary black (male) ideas about resistance. A close reading of his decision to protest against, rather than kill, the rogue white cop in his community underscores the possibilities of revamping black male gender roles. Adopting a nonviolent, self-sacrificial approach to black resistance, Socrates introduces the kind of gender revision and invention necessary to empower blacks generally and black men specifically to alter their social and economic circumstances.

Ultimately, *Breaking the Silence* seeks to uncover the cultural variables that reinforce patriarchy in the black community. Illuminating these variables is important, as it underscores how black coping mechanisms and strategies of survival can obscure black notions of womanhood and manhood. The need to identify the underlying problems of these gender models is especially crucial for black men because so many of us have become surrogate oppressors, venting out and displacing our masculine anxieties, frustrations, and rage onto black women. Unfortunately, many black women compound our victimizing patterns by becoming enabling agents, openly embracing self-sacrificial models of black womanhood that reify patriarchy. *Breaking the Silence* probes the sources and complexity of these interlocking gender and cultural dynamics as a path to developing new and useful approaches to black resistance. The first and most crucial step in developing these approaches is to identify the ways that blacks are, directly and indirectly, complicit in their own racial and gender oppression. Exposing these patterns of complicity will show that, despite our staggering social and economic disadvantages, we have the power to alter significant aspects of our racial and gender realities. The emotional, psychological, and material costs of ignoring complicity are far more than any of us can afford to pay.

LOVE JONES
A Black Male Feminist Critique of Chester Himes's
If He Hollers Let Him Go

IN WRITING HIS ESSAY "A Black Man's Place(s) in Feminist Criticism" Michael Awkward's chief aim was to legitimize black male perspectives on black women's literature. As discussed earlier, this was a daunting task, considering that most black male critics who engaged with black women's text were antagonistic, seeking, in most instances, to discredit unfavorable representations of black men. These chauvinistic and self-interested perspectives had led many black female feminists to conclude that black men were simply incapable of providing informed readings of black women's literature. Though acknowledging this troubling pattern, Awkward argues persuasively that critical perspective, not gender, should be the measuring stick of a black feminist methodology. Preoccupied, however, with legitimizing black men who critique black female texts, he does not adequately emphasize the potential role of black male feminists who engage black male texts. This oversight is crucial because it reinforces the idea that only black women deal with issues of gender. Given this reality, it becomes important for black male feminists to expand their range of critical inquiry to include how gender politics inform the works of black male authors. Such inquiries can provide new and useful insights into how black men construct their gender identities. They also can dispel prevailing assumptions about black women authors and intraracial gender issues.

By way of extending Awkward's theoretical project, I begin with a black male feminist critique of Chester Himes's *If He Hollers Let*

Him Go, a text that to date has not received a serious black feminist critique of any kind. Literary critics of *If He Hollers,* most of them black and male, typically characterize Bob Jones as a socially conscious Bigger Thomas. Most critics view Jones as the victim not only of white racism but of social emasculation at the hands of the black bourgeoisie and, more specifically, black and white women. From this perspective, Jones's peculiar socioeconomic circumstance *demands* he choose the lesser of two evils: either he marries his wealthy, self-absorbed, near-white fiancée Alice and accepts the "limitations" of his race, or he "rapes" Madge, a racially antagonizing white woman, to challenge white supremacy at the risk of death. For example, Gilbert Muller portrays Jones as "trapped in a menacing triangle involving Alice, who would domesticate him, and Madge, who would have him lynched" (27). Jones's personal freedom, writes Muller, is limited by his socioeconomic position: "Ironically Bob Jones, a middle-class intellectual, has been trapped by American culture as powerfully as the uneducated Bigger Thomas was in *Native Son.* In both novels, the configuration of race, class, caste, and gender *conspire* to render the protagonist in postures of guilt" (27; my italics).

Like Muller, Stephen Milliken argues that Alice and Madge are the chief antagonists in Bob Jones's struggle for equality. Milliken asserts, "Two women, one black and beautiful and the other white and vicious, are the principal barbed spurs that drive Bob Jones from point to point through his short and violent trajectory, as he is jabbed at or slashed first by one set of characters and then another" (77). Milliken characterizes Jones as a "kind of modern day Everyman" who refuses "every infringement on his full humanity, however 'little' the Alices of the world may consider him" (6). Jones's rebellious nature is deemed "manly" and his fate drawn as uncontrollable and tragic.

Echoing the image of Jones as a "modern day Everyman," Addison Gayle Jr. argues that *If He Hollers* is "concerned with the powerlessness of the black-middle-class intellectual" (182). Himes extends Richard Wright's social commentary, argues Gayle, to include a critique of class consciousness in the black community. Commending Himes for his staunch critique of black middle-class accommodationism, Gayle asserts, "American tyranny and oppression have been directed not only at Blacks of little education or financial standing, not only at the Bigger Thomases, but at the Bob Joneses as well. It is this lesson that the black middle class and their spokesmen, novelists, and critics have been unwilling to learn" (184–85). Gayle's only criticism of Jones, presented in revealing sexual language, is that he accepts the "right of society to castrate him" because he adheres to some "superficial values, as readily, though not as completely, as the Harrisons" (185).

These critical approaches fail to engage several issues that should be crucial to black male feminist criticism. To date, no critic has given adequate attention to the female voices in the text. As a result, none fully comprehends the degree to which Bob Jones is implicated in the white supremacist forces against which he ostensibly rebels. Paying attention to the women casts serious doubts on the consensus reading of Jones as a "Black Everyman." Milliken, for example (mis)represents the action of the novel when he explains Jones's pursuit of Madge at her apartment as a knee-jerk reaction to discovering that Alice is out with her white male colleague, Tom Leighton. Milliken ignores Jones's first unsuccessful trip to Madge's apartment. In fact, the only reason Alice is with Tom in the first place is that Jones has canceled their original plans so that he can pursue his sexual conquest of Madge. Typical of the ideological "blind spot" informing most criticism of *If He Hollers,* this demonstrates the pressing need for a black male feminist critique.

In their highly regarded biography *The Several Lives of Chester Himes,* Michel Fabre and Edward Margolies reveal that Himes's own misogynistic attitudes informed his rendering of women. *If He Hollers,* they note, was modeled in large part on Himes's own experiences in wartime Los Angeles. Himes openly resented the fact that his first wife, like the character Alice in the novel, flourished socially and economically in Los Angeles, while he, like Bob Jones, struggled to attain socioeconomic respectability. Clearly, some understanding of Himes's personal experiences and attitudes casts light on the tensions portrayed in *If He Hollers*. However, Bob Jones does not merely ventriloquize the personal racial-sexual politics of Chester Himes. Rather he brings into focus the anxieties about black masculinity shared by many black men of the World War II era and the subsequent Black Nationalist era of the 1960s and 1970s.

The crucial question that emerges is: Where does Bob Jones end and Chester Himes begin? While Jones should not be confused with Himes in any simplistic way, the unresolved aspects of the author's thought emerge most clearly in scenes involving Jones's interaction with black women. An investigation of Jones's investment in black masculinist discourse reveals tensions between Himes's conscious perspective and the implications of his text. In the opening scene of *If He Hollers*, Jones repudiates Ella Mae, his renter and ex-lover, for infantilizing him by providing him sexual favors out of social pity. He deems her "simpleminded, generous," and "sympathetic" like the black working-class theatergoers in the Lincoln theater who extend pity for a blind white acrobat rather than reserve it for themselves. Jones argues, "[T]he worse white folks treat us the more we love 'em. Ella Mae laying me because I wasn't married and she figured she had enough for me and Henry too; and a black audience clapping its hands off for a blind white acrobat" (6). The connection Jones makes between the black audience clapping for the blind white acrobat and Ella Mae having sex with him out of pity is strikingly incongruent. While it is clear that Jones's quarrel with the black working class stems from what he perceives as their willful participation in their own subjugation, it is unclear how his interpretation of their complicity is equivalent to his relationship with Ella Mae. Why, for instance, should she reserve her pity for herself rather than Jones? Aren't they both black and working class? How, then, does the significance of race, which is clearly the focal point of his blind-white-acrobat analogy, figure into his relationship with Ella Mae?

The link Jones makes between the two situations can best be explained as Himes's attempt to situate Ella Mae's sociopolitical misconduct beside the more clearly drawn self-effacing behavior of the black audience. Himes's equivocal comparison of Ella Mae to the black audience at the Lincoln reveals the complications, if not contradictions, of his rendering of her relationship with Jones. The reader is clearly encouraged to empathize with Jones and view Ella Mae as at once an unwitting participant in her own subjugation and a conscious conspirator in Jones's emasculation. Her "offense" against Jones, however, is never clearly delineated in the text. The assumptions of Himes's gendered argument follows this line of reasoning: The black woman's primary role is matriarch to the black family. As such, she provides physical and emotional nurturing to the black man when he is subjected to socioeconomic oppression. Her support, however, must accommodate his black masculine ethos; otherwise, she contributes *only* to his social denigration. When distilled, Ella Mae's "offense" is her unwillingness to assimilate a self-sacrificingly sexual or maternal subjectivity.

If Himes's characterization of Ella Mae is a subterfuge for Jones's (and his own) anxieties about masculinity, then it becomes clear why Jones's opening internal monologue about the increased racial tension in Los Angeles is interrupted by Ella Mae's crying newborn. The crying baby serves as the pivot point for Jones's transition of consciousness and as metaphor for his need for black female support. Seeking emotional comfort, he imagines changing places with the child: "Lucky little rascal, I thought, didn't know how lucky he was. I wish I had Ella Mae in bed with me; I could lose myself with her too" (5).

Although Jones's desire to "lose" himself with Ella Mae is ostensibly a desire to use sex as a temporary escape mechanism, his yearning to change places with the child reveals his need to be nurtured and protected by the black matriarch. The tension between Jones's need to be nurtured by black women and his desire to be recognized as a dominant patriarch contributes to his "crisis" of masculine identity. "Crisis" denotes the perpetual state of heightened anxiety Jones experiences in regards to the viability of his masculinity. His anxiety stems from the fear that he will never be able to measure up socially and economically to white men—in his view, the occupants of the ideal masculine space. Not unlike the real-life Chester Himes, Jones lets his struggle for social equality blind him to the elements of (white) patriarchy that necessitate sexual domination of the female. It is little wonder that Ella Mae's alleged (mis-)reading of Jones's need for sexual support as a need for motherly sympathy fuels his anxiety about his own masculinity. Denied full socioeconomic participation in white patriarchy, Jones, as a black man, can only exercise his masculinity through sexual conquest.

Arguably, Jones's conflict with Ella Mae has less to do with her pitying him than it does with his inability to articulate his feelings of powerlessness to her without appearing helpless. The fact that Jones provides no evidence that Ella Mae actually pities him bears this out. Because she does not respond remorsefully to his "punishment" of not speaking to her for a week, Jones concludes that she is aware she has offended him. He says, "When I found out she'd done it because she felt sorry for me I quit speaking to her for a week. But she hadn't let it bother her one way or the other" (5). Symptomatic of Jones's "crisis" of black masculinity, I argue, is a need for black women to acknowledge his sexual prowess. When Ella Mae does not acknowledge it—when in fact she "ignores" his reprimands altogether—Jones figures himself as a victim of both white supremacy and black female emasculation. Ella Mae confirms his suspicion that a social conspiracy of black women is leveled against him.

It is crucial that Himes presents only Jones's version of the relationship. The reader can only speculate about Ella Mae's perspective. Does she have sex with Jones out of pity or was she merely sexually attracted to him and acted in accord with momentary desire? Does she attach any political meaning to their relationship? Is sex for her simply a coping mechanism to deal with her reality as a black woman in a patriarchal society? Is her emotional detachment from Jones a way of guarding her own feelings?

Issues of class further complicate Himes's rendering of Jones's social emasculation at the hands of Alice, his affluent fiancée.

Jones initially describes Alice as a "really fine chick" whose near-white beauty gives him "personal pride." He is proud of the "appearance she made among white people; proud of what she demanded from white people, and the credit they gave her; and her position and prestige among her own people." While with her in public, he reflects, "I really felt like something." To Jones's thinking, Alice is the closest a black woman can come to feminine perfection without actually being white. The fundamental problem Jones perceives with his relationship with Alice is that her higher social status forces him to submit to her authority in ways that undermine his sense of his masculinity. When he reflects on the date Alice breaks with him, which precipitates his trip to the Lincoln theater, he thinks that had Susie, one of his working-class lovers, canceled a date with him at the last minute, he would not have tolerated it. Jones reflects that Alice had "called and said she ought to attend a sorority meeting she'd forgotten all about—she was president of the local chapter. And would I really mind? Of course I couldn't mind; that was where the social conventions had me. If she'd been Susie I could have said, 'Hell yes, I mind,' but I had to be a gentleman with Alice" (6–7).

Himes explicitly frames Jones's conflict with Alice as an inability to freely express his personal desires because of socioeconomic variables beyond his control. However, the comparison Jones makes between Alice and Susie reveals, when viewed from a black feminist perspective, the extent to which class informs black masculinist discourse. Jones implies that he can acquire sexual favors of Susie at his leisure. He clearly prefers Susie's deference toward him to Alice's dismissal. He attributes it to Susie's unpretentious nature, a nature determined by her class status. Closer investigation, however, reveals that Jones's preference for Susie is inextricably linked to her self-sacrificingly sexual attitude. Not surprisingly, Jones feels empowered in his relationship with her. As Awkward perceptibly argues, black women can only be *seen* by "black males-in-crisis" when they have been "subsumed by male desire(s)" and "emptied of subjectivity and selfhood" (20).

Alice, by virtue of her own will and social privilege, poses a formidable challenge to Jones's masculinity. Her middle-class standing, however, coupled with her physical attributes, promises Jones socioeconomic mobility. In stark contrast, Susie's pronounced selflessness poses no challenge to Jones's masculinity, but her class status promises little, if any, social prestige. As a member of the working class, Jones feels Alice's social status eclipses his "rightful" masculine space. Her class status and physical (white) beauty affords her the "privilege" of choosing from an elite number of prominent black men. Jones implies that, if he were to demand Alice treat him as Susie does, it would jeopardize his chances of marriage. His dilemma, although articulated as an inability to express true manhood, resides in his inability to fully subjugate Alice sexually, on the one hand, and attain the spoils of her social standing and beauty, on the other.

Jones clearly wants the prestige that comes with affiliation with someone of Alice's social caliber. His endurance of her capricious character is not a mark of his social emasculation at the hands of the black elite. Rather, it represents the extent to which he is willing to compromise his own integrity to attain social privilege. His constant references to the magnificence of Alice's white features bears this out. As she ascends the steps on their date to the white restaurant, Jones falls into a rapture: "[She] fell into the living room like Bette Davis, big-eyed and calisthenical and strictly sharp. She was togged in a flowing royal-purple chiffon evening gown with silver trimmings and a low square-cut neck that showed the tops of her creamy-white breasts with the darker disturbing seam down between . . . I gave her one look and caught an edge like a rash from head to foot, blinding and stinging. She was fine, fine, fine, so help me" (53). Clearly what marks Alice as "fine" for Jones is her resemblance to a glamorous white movie star.

Jones garners social currency when he is able to parade Alice in front of his friends. This becomes evident when Jones surprises Alice with dinner at an upscale white restaurant. Though he presents the dinner as a gift to Alice, Jones's purpose is clearly to place her on exhibit to acquire social currency for himself. When the white men in the restaurant begin to stare at Alice in admiration, Jones notes, "[S]he looked so poised and assured and beautiful, standing there among the white folks. I filled right up to the throat. I noticed a number of the white men sliding furtive glances of admiration at her, and I thought, 'You just go right on and keep yours, brothers, and I'll keep mine—and won't miss a thing either'" (58).

Given Jones's obvious preoccupation with whiteness, he might be expected to understand why Alice passes as white when she goes to such restaurants. However, when she informs Jones that her embarrassment in the restaurant stems from her awareness that white people know "just what we are" (60), he becomes infuriated and condemns her for being embarrassed to be black. Later that same evening, after a traumatic encounter with racist policemen, Jones continues to chide Alice. While sitting on the beachfront, he asks her if she is "just finding out" she is "a nigger?" (64). Jones's critique of white oppression is radically gendered. For him, using Alice as a social commodity to impress whites is a viable mode of resistance. When Alice utilizes her own ability to pass for similar purposes, however, Jones views her actions as racially reprehensible. Neither Jones nor the novel itself offers any space to imagine women employing modes of co-option or resistance to white supremacy. As a result, black female agency is presented as emasculating to black men.

This double standard is also made manifest in Jones's response to Alice's implied lesbian encounters and sexual relations with white men. Despite his own numerous sexual indiscretions, including one with a white woman, Jones condemns Alice for what he perceives as her socio-sexual arrogance and corruption. When Jones is first introduced to Tom Leighton, he immediately suspects Alice of having an affair with him. He conjectures, "She might be having an affair with Leighton sure enough, I thought. She wouldn't count that, just like she wouldn't count that stuff at Stella's. She'd probably be proud of it, I thought; probably feel that I shouldn't resent it even if I found out" (87). That Jones engages in sexual affairs with other women has no bearing on his rendering of Alice's moral character. What marks her alleged sexual behavior as morally/socially reprehensible is its socioeconomic relationship to black patriarchy. To Jones's way of thinking, black female sex with white men is socially debilitating for black men because it calls attention to their socioeconomic impotence. Operating on an uneven playing field, black men cannot compete sexually with white men for (black and white) female acquisition/domination.

When Jones happens upon Alice and Leighton, shortly after returning from his failed rendezvous with Madge, he becomes enraged and articulates his socio-sexual anxieties about white men and black women. He reflects angrily, "It really galled me to have a white guy take my girl out on a date. I wouldn't have minded so much if he had been the sharpest, richest, most important coloured guy in the world; I'd have still felt I could compete. But a white guy had his colour—I couldn't compete with that. It was all up to the chick—if she liked white, I didn't have a chance; if she didn't, I didn't have anything to worry about. But I'd have to know, and I didn't know about Alice" (142).

Jones's rendering of white privilege places the black female in a curious relationship to power. In short, hers is the power to choose the mate of her choice. Given that the social odds are stacked against black men, all they can do is hope black women do not "like white." Jones's view of black female "privilege" conspicuously ignores the exploitive dynamic traditionally informing relationships between white men and black women. Further, it collapses class and caste distinctions among black women to accommodate a black male-centered discourse that renders invisible the gender privilege black men have historically exercised over black women.

At points, Jones seems to sense the contradictions in his own understanding. He is aware, for instance, that even if he marries Alice, his access to the spoils of white patriarchy will still be limited by race. Himes amplifies Jones's awareness of his own contradictions, I argue, to demonstrate the "Catch-22" dynamic of white supremacy. Jones's "choices," either to marry Alice or rape Madge, provide him no consolation because both require acquiescence to white supremacist ideology. Ultimately, Himes argues that black (male) self-determinacy is impossible in a white supremacist society. A black male feminist approach, however, reveals that Jones's social dilemma is informed by his deep investment in both white patriarchy and middle-class values. The extent of Jones's investment is brought to the fore the morning after his unsuccessful attempt at a sexual conquest of Madge. He dreams of a black man who attempts to kill an unarmed white man with a large knife. The dream highlights the black man's inability to wound his white enemy. Although appearing helpless, the white man actually maintains the upper hand. His appearance of helplessness is in fact a façade he uses to lure the black man closer in order to murder him. By the time the black man realizes that the white man wields a concealed weapon, the damage has been done and the only option he has is to flee for his life. After Jones wakes from this dream, he reflects on the limitations of his socioeconomic mobility. Aware that most black people would consider him "a lucky black boy" because he has the potential to become an "important Negro," he responds, "If you couldn't swing down Hollywood Boulevard and know that you belonged; if you couldn't make a polite pass at Lana Turner at Ciro's without having the gendarmes beat the black off you for getting out of your place; if you couldn't eat a thirty-dollar dinner at an hotel without choking on the insults, being a great big 'Mister' nigger didn't mean a thing." Jones's ostensible desire is to be "accepted as a man . . .without ambition, without distinction, either of race, creed, or colour; just a simple Joe" who can walk "down an American street . . . without any other identifying characteristics but weight, height, and gender" (153).

There are striking contradictions in Jones's rendering of the black middle-class ethos and his notion of white privilege that call into question his claim that all he wants is to be a "simple Joe." What he finds unacceptable about the black middle class is not their wealth, power, or prestige—characteristics that draw him to

Alice in the first place—but their willingness to be satisfied with high social standing that is *limited* to the black community. From Jones's perspective, if whites do not respect the black middle class, prestige in the black community is rendered meaningless. To this end, the social position of an average working-class white man—because he is judged on merit alone—is more desirable than that of a wealthy black professional. Jones's ostensible desire for simple equality, however, is belied by his idea of what constitutes equality. The privileges he values—to eat at expensive restaurants and rub shoulders with the white, rich, and famous—are informed by a middle-class ethos. Jones desires far more than just to be a black everyman or a "simple Joe." He wants both the social privileges that come with being a white male and the socioeconomic mobility that comes with being wealthy. That he is blind to this aspect of his character throws his rendering of the black middle class and white society radically into question.

Refocusing with the black women's perspective in the foreground reveals the gendered assumptions underpinning Himes's black masculine discourse. His text provides a clear case of what Deborah King calls "monist" black politics. To black male monist thinking, the end of black male oppression will necessarily precipitate an end to all oppressions, including sexism. Thus any attempt by black women to vocalize the specific intraracial gender oppression of black men is interpreted not only as compromising racial solidarity but as emasculating black men. Black female oppression becomes subsumed within the totalizing, gendered discourse of black oppression. Black male oppression, then, masquerades as the oppression of all black people.

The monist substructure of Himes's text subsumes black female oppression within a veiled black masculine discourse, thereby precluding consideration of the black man as victimizer of black women. To date, no critic has taken Himes to task for his phallocentric rendering of his black female characters. The women continue to be relegated to the margins of criticism and elided from serious consideration. To demonstrate the usefulness of such a black male feminist perspective, I will consider Ella Mae's critique of Jones as it relates to his internalization of white (male) supremacist ideology, on the one hand, and his investment in monist reasoning to resist this same ideology, on the other. Her perspective on Jones points directly to the difficulty of constructing a program of resistance in a monist system.

Ella Mae's dialogue with Jones prior to his date with Alice at the upscale white restaurant underscores the contradictions in his racial politics. After Jones takes an extended shower, Ella Mae says, "You oughta be clean enough even for Alice now—two baths in one day." Jones replies jokingly, "I'm tryna turn white." Undeterred by his jocularity, Ella Mae continues to press the point. "I wouldn't be s'prised none," she chides, "'lil as it's said." Clearly unnerved by Ella Mae's insinuations, Jones, unable to "let it go," continues his course of signifying. "You know how much I love the white folks," he says. "You just ain't saying it, either," Ella Mae retorts. "All that talking you do 'bout 'em all the time. I see you got the whitest coloured girl you could find" (47).

When Ella Mae extends her critique to include Jones's selection of a "rich and light and almost white" girl in Alice, he becomes defensive and accuses her of acting "like a black gal." To act "like a black gal" is for Jones to attack black men who are striving to improve their socioeconomic condition. It is also for darker-skinned women to purposely misrepresent the social dynamics informing the relationship between black men and white or fairer-skinned women as a mode of control. It makes sense, the narrative suggests, that black men would gravitate toward white and faired-skinned women, given the abrupt nature of darker-skinned women. It is out of racial jealousy, then, and not political insight that Ella Mae condemns Jones.

Closer investigation reveals that Jones is wedded to notions of white beauty. Even as he consciously grapples with various elements of white supremacy, he never fully addresses his desire for white and fairer-skinned women. Because Jones thinks that darker-skinned black women are incapable of evaluating the taboos existing between black men and white/light women, he can dismiss Ella Mae's appraisal of his relationship with Alice altogether. In fact, Jones displaces his anxiety about his own internalization of white supremacy onto Ella Mae. "Okay, baby, I quit," Jones finally concedes, and then reflects, "I wondered what was eating her" (47). Later, in the company of the black female social workers at Alice's house, Jones makes a similar assessment of Cleo, one of the darker-skinned social workers. When she states she does not understand why prominent black men choose to marry "white tramps" over black women of comparable social standing, Jones remarks, "You wouldn't [understand]. . . as black as you are" (85). To be darker skinned, for Jones, is clearly to be less desirable sexually and socially than light and white women.

The intensity and depth of Ella Mae's critique makes clear Himes's awareness, on some level, of his protagonist's investment in white supremacist ideology. That Jones is clearly taken aback by Ella Mae's accusations of his wanting to be white reveals that her accusations have an impact on him. The question emerges: What is Himes attempting to convey about Jones and Ella Mae in this scene? The few critics who address Ella Mae's role in the novel describe her behavior toward Jones as the jealous reaction of an ex-lover. Himes's own perspective regarding the white woman/ black man taboo definitely supports this reading. In his autobiography, My Life of Absurdity, he accuses black women and white men of throwing "me into the arms of white women, who were eager enough to hold me" (34–35). This telling comment reveals the extent to which Himes considered the pursuit of white women by black men symptomatic of both black women's hostility toward black men and white male oppression. Jones's refusal, then, to seriously engage Ella Mae's accusation of his preference for white and light-skinned women can be read as Himes's attempt to underscore the sexual tensions still existing between the two ex-lovers—namely, Ella Mae's desire to rekindle the relationship with Jones. Her critical appraisal of Jones's penchant for light and white women is framed as a political ploy to retain his affection.

More evidence of Himes's monist politics is revealed in Jones's interaction with Alice shortly after he tells her of his demotion. When attempting to explain to Alice why he retaliates in kind to Madge's racial slur, Jones becomes frustrated because Alice's only concern is for him to reinstate himself in the company. She wants him to apologize to Madge because in her view Madge's insult was "such a little thing." Lamenting Alice's ultimatum to either apologize to Madge or risk losing her, Jones reflects, "I didn't have a choice" (99). In a dream sequence immediately following this exchange, Jones finds himself chasing after Alice, who is screaming for help in a wooded area. Armed with a ".45-calibre short-barreled revolver" so large that in order to hide it he has to stuff it in his trousers, Jones arrives at the scene only to find that Alice has been dwarfed into "a little rag doll." When Jones looks up from the little doll, he sees, leaning on the fence, "millions of white women . . . looking at me, giving me the most sympathetic smiles I ever saw." Awaking from the dream, he feels "absolute impotence," until he begins thinking about Madge. Even as he expresses his contempt for her, his sexual language implies his desire to seduce her. He reflects, "Memory of my fight with Alice came back, and then I saw Madge's kidney-shaped mouth, brutal at the edges, spitting out the word 'nigger' and something took a heavy hammer and nailed me to the bed" (101).

The salient sexual imagery in this dream sequence supports Himes's misgivings about black women who criticize black men, like Jones, who pursue relationships with white women. Jones's oversized phallus, represented by the sawed off revolver that he fails to adequately conceal beneath his trousers, reveals at once his dangerous potential as an oppressed black man and the limits of that potential demonstrated by the inability of his "gun" to harm the yellow-tusked swine that threaten to harm Alice. Jones's gaze from the full-sized white women on the fence to the dead, little Alice "rag doll" in his hand, and then back to the fence, calls attention to disparity in size and number between Alice and the white women. His gaze suggests that he has wasted valuable energies pursuing Alice's affection. She is, in fact, a poor substitute for the "real" women on the fence. Their sympathetic smiles, set against Alice's unsparing remarks to Jones the previous day, reinforce Himes's thinking about black men who actively pursue white women. Ultimately, the dream confirms that emasculating black women compel black men to seek out sympathetic partners in white women. It also foreshadows Jones's sexual pursuit of Madge.

Ella Mae's conversation with Jones the night he plans his rendezvous with Madge underscores the black male cultural narratives that inform Jones's choice of Madge over Alice. After taking a shower and getting dressed, Jones "jokes" with Ella Mae that he is "going out with" a "white chick tonight." Cognizant of his preoccupation with whiteness, Ella Mae retorts, "[Y]ou're saying it for a joke . . . but I believe you, you're just the type." As he had in his earlier dialogue with Ella Mae, Jones tries to defuse her suspicion with jocular prompting. He replies, "You know I like my white women, baby . . . Couldn't get along with without 'em." Undeterred by his banter, Ella Mae returns, "You just like all the niggers. . . Get a white woman and go from Cadillacs to cotton sacks" (137).

Embedded in Ella Mae's reply are several cultural narratives of black male social progress. Because many black men were systematically denied access to property ownership for much of the first half of the century, ownership of expensive cars, specifically Cadillacs, became a marker of success. That Jones covets his '42 Buick Roadmaster because he knows "rich white folks out in Beverly couldn't even buy a new car now" (10) speaks directly to this dynamic. Like expensive automobiles, relationships with white woman were also viewed as material markers of black male success. Many affluent black men would abandon black women of their own class to marry or date white women of lower social standing. For example, Peaches, a black female worker on Jones's crew, notes, "If a coloured girl asks one of you niggers to take her to the show you start grumbling 'bout money—liable to even ask her to pay the way. And then the raggedest-looking old beat-up white tramp can come by and get your whole paycheck. You dump like a dump truck" (134). Most crucially, Ella Mae's and Peaches's assessment of the socially and morally retrogressive nature of the black men/white women relationship bears itself out in Jones's eventual choice of Madge over Alice.

Even as Himes discounts the black female voices in the text, he infuses an argument in Jones's narrative to circumvent (white) readings of Jones's attraction to Madge as inherently primitive. In an extended internal monologue, Jones enumerates a litany of sexual exploits with "good" white women from his past. He thinks, "I had known white girls in both California and Ohio. I had gone with a little Italian girl in Cleveland for almost a year. Then there had been a tall brown-haired girl who worked as a stenographer in a downtown office who used to let me take her out now and then . . . Both of them were good girls, as good morally as most." He concludes, "So it wasn't that Madge was white; it was the way she used it. She had a sign up in front of her as big as the Civic Center—KEEP AWAY, NIGGERS, I'M WHITE! And without having to say one word she could keep all the white men in the world feeling they had to protect her from black rapists. That made her doubly dangerous because she thought about Negro men" (125).

Himes amplifies the sexual-racial intensity between Madge and Jones by highlighting Madge's social standing as an uneducated, middle-aged, poor, single woman. In stark contrast, Jones is an up-and-coming professional who has several years of college training and a promising future. When he is demoted from leaderman to machinist for retaliating in kind to Madge's racial slurs, his hate/lust of her is exacerbated by his awareness that "[a]ll she had was her colour" (179). It is precisely because she lacks social status that her whiteness is amplified. In short, her only means of power is her relationship to white men as the paragon of white virtue. Jones feels that she understands this dynamic and uses it to exert her racial power over him. What Jones ostensibly wants to do is force her to submit to him sexually as a way to recuperate his lost manhood and challenge white supremacy. At one point Jones thinks that if he could "just get over the notion [that] women were the same, black and white" (130) he could transcend his fear of white power and sexually dominate Madge.

The politics of racial resistance that inform Jones's dilemma with Madge obscure the phallocentric underpinnings of his rationale. His sexual conquest of Madge is framed as an ideological challenge to white supremacy, which, on some level, he is aware he has internalized. Thus Jones experiences his desire to sexually dominate Madge as an attempt to overturn the belief that white women are by nature more beautiful and sexually desirable than black women. Moreover, to "corrupt" the white female is for Jones to resist the tenets of white supremacy and empty white patriarchy of its socio-psychological potency. A black male feminist perspective, however, calls attention to the contradictions implicit in Jones's program of resistance. To frame a strategy of resistance in terms of a patriarchal ethos dependent upon female domination is clearly problematic. Its most debilitating effect is the erasure of the experience of racism and sexism for black women. Jones's attempts to subvert the white patriarchal system by inverting the power dynamic serve only to reinscribe phallocentric notions of power and control. The female body as commodity remains the site where masculinity is negotiated.

Many unresolved tensions echo throughout *If He Hollers*. Most crucially, the text foregrounds the black man's inability to subvert the white patriarchal discourse without at once substantiating mythologies of black primitivism. A black male feminist criticism reveals that such tensions remain unresolved precisely because the black male discourse frames itself ideologically within the contours of white masculinity. Bob Jones, and to a disturbing extent Chester Himes, could not imagine subverting white supremacy without domination of the white female body. Given that focus, black women are simply invisible, their voices silenced or misunderstood. Ella Mae's suspicion that Jones in fact wanted to be white appears all the more relevant in light of his total inability to hear her.

The long-standing tradition of phallocentric criticism of the novel reveals the extent to which black monist racial reasoning—now under serious interrogation by black feminists like Deborah King—has informed black (male) criticism. Little wonder why Ella Mae, who provides the most astute criticism of Jones, has been ignored by literary critics as well as by Jones; or, that Alice's experiences of racism and sexism have never been at issue. If, as Valerie Smith argues, the most important contribution black men can make to the feminist project is through an investigation of "the way constructions of masculinity affect the experience of race, and the way that connection is represented in literature" (496), black men must rigorously engage the gender politics informing black male texts. Most central black male figures in the African American literary canon—Frederick Douglass, Charles Chesnutt, Paul Lawrence Dunbar, W. E. B. Du Bois, Ralph Ellison, James Weldon Johnson, Wallace Thurman, and Ernest Gaines—have received either cursory attention in regard to their gendered politics or none at all. Unfortunately, black women—who have written most of the feminist criticism available on these important writers—have had little success in recruiting black men for this endeavor.

If black male critics are to be useful and productive to the black feminist project—to enhancing the discourse on African American literature in general—they must stop policing black male borders and take the lion's share of the burden of redressing phallocentric readings of black-male-authored texts. Black feminists, Awkward rightly argues, have set the precedence for such revisioning of black masculinity. Before black men can productively engage black feminists on the issue of black masculinity, however, they must accept that their victimization in America as black men does not exempt them from participation in patriarchy. The dismantling of patriarchy is no more the sole responsibility of black women than is the dismantling of white supremacy in America the sole responsibility of black people. To echo the words of Toni Morrison, when black men and women write as critics and authors, "all necks are on the line" (397).

2

BLACK PATRIARCHY AND THE DILEMMA
OF BLACK WOMEN'S COMPLICITY IN JAMES
BALDWIN'S *GO TELL IT ON THE MOUNTAIN*

JAMES BALDWIN HAS TAKEN fire on his gender politics from two directions. In *Soul on Ice* (1968) Eldridge Cleaver asserts that Baldwin's homosexuality renders him unfit to address the concerns of black men. In *Black Women in the Fiction of James Baldwin* (1985) Trudier Harris contends that Baldwin's investment in black patriarchy renders him unfit to address the concerns of black women. In fact, Baldwin makes significant contributions to intraracial gender debates in *Go Tell It on the Mountain* (1953) that explode both claims against him. Highlighting the social consequences of black patriarchy, Baldwin draws critical attention to the disparities of power between men and women in the black community. Specifically, he shows how victim status enables black men to skirt responsibility for oppressing black women. Gabriel will not own up to his domination of black women because he views himself as the chief victim of white oppression and the burden-bearer of his family. Saddled with these social challenges as a man, he feels entitled to black women's self-sacrifice and deference. Thus he confuses dominating black women with affirming his manhood.

Baldwin's engagement with Gabriel and patriarchy is important from a black male feminist perspective because he casts light on the process by which black men rationalize their domination of black women. In doing so, he makes explicit the problematic notions of black manhood that inform Himes's treatment of Bob Jones and manhood in *If He Hollers* (1945). Himes uses black women as political "props" to generate sympathy for black male suffering. He does so by grouping black women with whites in the emasculation of black men, a tactic that encourages the reader to dismiss black women's perspectives on suffering and black men. In contrast, Baldwin treats black women as complex individuals who—like their male counterparts—struggle to come to terms with the realities of their subordinate social status. More importantly, he accounts for the ways that black women are oppressed as women within the patriarchal structure of black community. Though Himes's *If He Hollers* includes black women's protests against black male abuses, he presents those protests as self-serving and spiteful. As a result, women that speak out against patriarchy appear as emasculators. Their perceived betrayal reinforces the ideas that Jones is the true victim of white oppression and that black women lack the credibility to accuse black men of abuse.

In *Go Tell It* Baldwin recovers the experiences of black women's oppression that are omitted in Himes's portrait of Bob Jones and black emasculation. Specifically, he disrupts the victimization discourse that allows black men like Jones and Gabriel to explain away their subjection of black women as a direct result of white oppression. By disrupting this victimization discourse he encourages the reader to empathize with black women's suffering at the hands of black men. Elizabeth and Florence do not appear as emasculators when they recount episodes of black male victimization because *Go Tell It* establishes black patriarchy as a pervasive and oppressive force in black women's lives. What becomes clear thematically is that to dominate black women in the name of affirming manhood is to actively participate in oppression. Therefore, women who fight against patriarchy are not participants in emasculation but revolutionaries deserving of admiration.

In *Go Tell It* Baldwin also provides a useful model for understanding the effects of internalized patriarchy for black women. He shows how women unknowingly support patriarchy in their relationships with men and examines the social obstacles that prevent most women from breaking free of this complicity. Elizabeth endures domestic violence and verbal abuse because she feels indebted to Gabriel for marrying her and adopting her "bastard" son John. Her feelings of gratitude bolster Gabriel's distorted perspective on morality and manhood, allowing him to dominate her without experiencing any feelings of guilt or remorse. By enduring abuse in the name of gratitude, Elizabeth indirectly affirms patriarchy and contributes to her own suffering. Florence is not as easily pacified. She represents the only hope for breaking free of complicity. Though burdened by the pressure to support patriarchy, she manages to defy her brother's authority at home and in the church. Her biggest obstacle is that she lacks a supportive community to validate her experiences of patriarchal abuse. Thus, she is forced in times of physical and emotional crisis to turn to the black church for support—an institution that endorses and polices the patriarchal system that she openly repudiates. The only way out of complicity is for Florence to cultivate a new community. Though Baldwin suggests that community-building is possible in Florence's relationship with John, he leaves the outcome of her pursuits open to question. His open-ended conclusion does not portend failure, however. Florence takes a bold verbal stance against her tyrannical and abusive brother at the end of the novel despite overwhelming pressures to remain silent. If she continues to progress in this direction toward empowerment, she will likely find the strength to triumph over her brother and patriarchy.

In *Soul on Ice* Cleaver staunchly defends the black patriarchal structure under scrutiny in *Go Tell It*. In particular, he discounts Baldwin's insights on black men because he views homosexuality as a pathology that stems from white emasculation on the one hand and a suppressed desire to assimilate on the other. Baldwin cannot be trusted to represent black men properly in fiction because his pathology causes him to idealize whiteness and to turn "the razor edge of hatred against 'blackness'—upon himself, what he is, and all those who look like him [. . . and] remind him of himself" (129). Cleaver insists that the only cultural insight that can be gleaned from Baldwin's fiction is the extent to which assimilated black men are willing to go to appease their white male oppressors. Thus to read his fiction is to experience an aberrant depiction of black manhood that operates in the service of white oppression rather than that of black male empowerment.

Whereas Cleaver condemns Baldwin for misrepresenting black men, Harris attacks him precisely for his uncritical view of black womanhood. Specifically, she takes issue with Baldwin's portraits of emotionally battered black women. She argues that he reinforces the black male status quo by creating women characters who rely solely on men to affirm their womanhood and to assess their social value: "It is a function of their guilt as well as of their creation that most of the black female characters in Baldwin's fiction have been subordinated to the males: they are in a supportive, *serving* position in relation to the males and the male images in their lives . . . [T]hey are incomplete without men or male images in their lives because wholeness without males is not a concept the majority of them have internalized" (9). Harris concludes that Baldwin's depictions of black women are irredeemably flawed because he cannot envision a social or political space outside the domain of patriarchal subjectivity. In this regard, his fiction reconstitutes the kind of problematic gender norms that allow black men to oppress black women with impunity.

Operating as they do from static notions of gender roles and empowerment, Cleaver and Harris base their arguments against Baldwin on problematic gender and cultural standards. Both judge Baldwin to be unfit because he does not conform to their essentialist notions. The end result becomes a critical analysis of his personal qualifications, rather than a productive and useful exploration of his literary engagement with gender politics.

In effect, *Go Tell It* carves out a critique of gender politics which reveals the limitations of Cleaver's and Harris's arguments. Baldwin does not create characters that are stereotypes. Rather he creates complex characters who transcend labels and who contend with real social challenges that cannot be easily resolved. Even though Gabriel dominates his wife and children and enjoys institutional support for patriarchy, he is still deeply conflicted about his manhood and morality. Florence is acutely aware that she is a victim of patriarchy. Yet her awareness does not alleviate the guilt she feels toward her mother, whose patriarchal ideas she rejects and whom she leaves on her deathbed in order to pursue a better life in the North. Elizabeth recognizes that Richard's suicide was brought about by his false imprisonment and humiliation at the hands of corrupt white policemen, but she still agonizes over whether she could have prevented his death with news of her pregnancy.

To impose rigid gender standards onto *Go Tell It* is to devalue Baldwin's project. He is not concerned with rehearsing conventional notions of manhood and patriarchy, but rather with exploring new possibilities for understanding these issues. In *Notes of a Native Son* he writes, "I think all theories are suspect, that the finest principles may have to be modified, or may even be pulverized by the demands of life, and that one must find, therefore, one's own moral center and move through the world hoping that this center will guide one aright" (9). In "Freaks and the American Ideal of Manhood," he notes that he is thankful that "all of the American categories of male and female, straight or not, black or white, were shattered . . . very early in my life. Not without anguish, certainly; but once you have discerned the meaning of a label, it may seem to define you for others, but it does not have the power to define you to yourself" (819). While his maverick positions on gender, race, and cultural issues came at a high social cost—making him an easy target for homophobic black nationalists like Cleaver and hard-line feminists like Harris—they helped pave the way for important and necessary investigations into black patriarchy.

In *Go Tell It* Baldwin illuminates the problems of victim status for black men in his depiction of Gabriel's response to Roy's serious injury at the hands of a white gang. Rather than acknowledge that Roy instigated the fight in which he is stabbed, Gabriel tries to make his son out to be the victim of racial violence and poor mothering. He feels that his wife, Elizabeth, is ultimately to blame for the incident because she fails in her womanly duties to supervise the children in his absence. While carefully tending to Roy's wounds, he rants accusatorily, "I'm sure going to be having some questions to ask you in a minute, old lady. I'm going to be wanting to know just how come you let this boy go out and get half killed" (43). When Florence intervenes, emphasizing that Roy rather than Elizabeth is ultimately to blame, Gabriel reveals his gendered expectations of social entitlements: "I'm out of this house . . . every day the Lord sends, working to put the food in these children's mouths. Don't you think I got a *right* to ask the mother of these children to look after them and see that they don't break their necks before I get back home?" (47; my emphasis).

Here Baldwin shows how victim status allows black men to skirt responsibility for rearing their children. Gabriel has the "right" to blame Elizabeth for Roy's injuries because cultural and social expectations assign her full responsibility for homemaking and care giving. His position of criticism is further bolstered because—unlike many black men—he provides adequate financial support for his family. In cultural terms, Gabriel is a "good black man," meaning that he has acquired additional cultural distinction as a man because he has managed to "beat the racial odds" by avoiding the pitfalls of drugs and imprisonment, and because he accepts "responsibility" for his wife and children. He clearly understands his status, which becomes apparent by the nature and tone of the rhetorical question he puts to Florence, insinuating that he rather than Elizabeth is shouldering disproportionate responsibility for taking care of the family.

Gabriel's bias is clear when he invokes the memory of his mother to reinforce his accusations against Elizabeth. When she defends herself by noting that Roy's behavior is "exactly" like his daddy's, Gabriel rants, "I reckon you know . . . all about a mother's love. I sure reckon on you telling me how a woman can sit in the house all day and let her own flesh and blood go out and get half butchered. Don't tell me you don't know no way to stop him, because I remember my mother, God rest her soul, and she'd have found a way" (47).

When Baldwin has Gabriel invoke his mother as the model of ideal black womanhood he draws attention to the expectation of black women's self-sacrifice to men and their families. Most important, he maps out the ways that black women become policing agents for patriarchy. Gabriel's relationship with his mother is crucial in this regard because she rears him to believe that as a man he should expect black women to cater to his every emotional, physical, and material desire. Baldwin casts light on a crucial source of patriarchal entitlement during Florence's reflections in prayer:

> There was only one future in that house, and it was Gabriel's— to which, since Gabriel was a manchild, all else must be sacrificed. Her mother did not, indeed, think of it as sacrifice, but as logic: Florence was a girl, and would by and by be married, and have children of her own, and all the duties of a woman; and this being so, her life in the cave was the best possible preparation for her future life. But Gabriel was a man; he would go out one day into the world to do a man's work, and he needed, therefore, meat when there was any in the house, and clothes, whenever clothes could be bought, and the strong indulgence of his womenfolk, so that he would know how to be with women when he had a wife. And he needed the education that Florence desired far more than he, and that she might have gotten had he not been born. It was Gabriel who was slapped and scrubbed each morning and sent off to the one-room schoolhouse—which he hated, and where he managed to learn, so far as Florence could discover, almost nothing at all. (72–73)

Florence's account of Gabriel's gender-privileged upbringing explains in part why he experiences little guilt for his cruel behavior toward women. Encouraged by his mother to view himself both as the burden bearer and leader of the black family, he experiences his mistreatment of women from the vantage point of the victimized, not the victimizer. His mother reinforces his victim status in her treatment of Florence, denying her equal attention and resources because she thinks that women have the much easier path in life; they need only find a husband to ensure personal happiness and financial security. This problematic perception of gender roles provides insights into why Gabriel is able, with good conscience, to blame women for his own destructive behavior. Believing himself always to be the victim, he has little comprehension of the suffering of others, the only exception being Royal, whom he tries to mold into his own image.

The problems of Gabriel's patriarchal thinking are illuminated in his theology, especially when he links Elizabeth's "unrepented" sin of fornication to Roy's uncontrollable behavior. Gabriel reveals his feelings as he watches Elizabeth and John kneel before the altar later on the same day following the incident with Roy: "[I]t came to him that this living son, this headlong, living Royal, might be cursed for the sin of his mother, whose sin had never been truly repented; for that the living proof of her sin, he who knelt tonight, a very interloper among the saints, stood between her soul and God" (114–15). Tellingly, Gabriel arrives at this conclusion after he considers, then dismisses, the possibility that God is punishing him through Roy for the way that he abandoned Esther and his first son Royal during their greatest time of need. Though he acknowledges his role in their fates only to Deborah—and only after she learns the truth on her own—he believes that he has adequately addressed the matter and that God has forgiven him. He believes that he is innocent of wrongdoing despite the fact that he has deliberately withheld knowledge of his first son from Elizabeth that would expose the hypocrisy of his accusations against her.

Gabriel's preoccupation with Elizabeth's sin—his frustration that she shows no regret for conceiving John out of wedlock—stems largely from his need to control her through shaming. Baldwin underscores the problems of his patriarchal theology through Elizabeth in the heated conversation over Roy's injuries. Identifying the underlying motives of Gabriel's accusations against her, she protests, "I don't know how in the world you expect me to run this house, and look after these children, and keep running around the block after Roy. *No, I can't stop him, I done told you that, and you can't stop him neither. You don't know what to do with this boy, and that's why you all the time trying to fix the blame on somebody*" (47; italics in text). Elizabeth recognizes that Gabriel's accusations against her cover his own feelings of parental confusion. Blaming Roy's misbehavior on poor mothering, Gabriel does not have to claim his responsibility in the matter, nor does he have to admit to being perplexed, like the women, over Roy's actions.

Gabriel's patriarchal theology explains why he is unable to appreciate Elizabeth's affection for John. Her guiltless love for him runs counter to all that Gabriel has been taught in the church and elsewhere about gender roles and the importance of marriage to patriarchy. From his vantage point, he has "rescued" Elizabeth—like Deborah before her—from a life of social ridicule through marriage. It would seem logical to him that Elizabeth would want to erase the existence of her firstborn if she could, especially given the stigmas that such practices carry for women. That she does not means for Gabriel that she is unappreciative of the "sacrifice" that he made by marrying her in the first place. He experiences these feelings of patriarchal resentment, however, within a religious context, viewing her refusal to admit regret as a sign of her unwillingness to embrace fully Christian doctrine—an unwillingness that is bringing God's wrath upon his family.

Given the ways that patriarchy informs Gabriel's theology, it is not surprising that he feels empowered to strike Elizabeth whenever she tries to defend herself against his accusations. He views himself as the ordained "head of his household" and approaches any challenges to his authority as spiritual treason—a mind-set that empowers him to resort to whatever measures he deems appropriate to maintain "order in his house." Baldwin allows us to see, however, that his violence against Elizabeth stems from the biting accuracy of her defense and from the fact that she defends herself in front of Florence and the children. Lacking the words to refute Elizabeth's claims, Gabriel responds with brute force, the only way that he knows to regain control of the situation and demonstrate that he is still in charge.

Read intertextually, Baldwin's rendering of Gabriel invokes Zora Neale Hurston's rendering of Joe Starks in *Their Eyes Were Watching God* (1937), the Ur-text of feminist and black feminist studies. To conceal his anxieties about aging and manhood, Joe berates his younger and attractive wife Janie. On one occasion, however, when he belittles her in front a group of townsmen, she rebels like Elizabeth, and addresses the real motives for his attacks on her appearance: "Naw, Ah ain't no young gal no mo' but den Ah ain't no old woman neither. Ah reckon Ah looks mah age too. But Ah'm uh woman every inch of me, and Ah know it. Dat's uh whole lot more'n you kin say. You big-bellies round here and put out a lot of brag, but 'tain't nothin' to it but yo' big voice. Humph! Talkin' 'bout me lookin' old! When you pull down yo' britches, you look lak de change uh life" (75). Hurston brings the political significance of this scene into focus, writing that Janie's comments "had robbed [Joe] of his illusion of irresistible maleness that all men cherish, which was terrible . . . But Janie had done worse, she had cast down his empty armor before men and they had laughed, would keep on laughing" (75). Janie exposes Joe's masculine vulnerabilities because she refuses the role of obedient and faithful wife. Her refusal unnerves Joe because he understands on some level that the maintenance of his patriarchal authority is dependent upon his wife's complicity of silence. When she breaks the silence expected of her as obedient wife, she unveils the limitations of his authority over her. She also opens him to ridicule by his male peers because she demonstrates that he has lost his ability to control his wife, a telling sign to the townsmen that his manhood is in serious jeopardy. Lige Moss's teasing remarks bring these patriarchal dynamics starkly into focus. He tells Joe, "Ah ruther be shot with tacks than tuh hear dat 'bout mahself" (75). The insult is especially crushing to Joe because he has grown accustomed to being admired and envied by other men for possessing wealth, power, and a beautiful wife. Having lost the respect of his peers, he knows that "[w]hen he parad[es] his [material] possessions, hereafter, they w[ill] not consider the two [manhood and wealth] together.

They'd look with envy at the things and pity the man that owned them" (75). Convinced, like Gabriel, that he is entitled as a husband to his wife's obedience and servility, he experiences intense feelings of betrayal and emasculation. When he physically assaults Janie he does so believing that his actions are warranted because she exposes his weaknesses "in the eyes of other men" (76). He remains oblivious to his culpability in Janie's suffering because he perceives his abusive behavior as a patriarchal entitlement. This reveals why he characterizes Janie's comments as "cruel" and "deceitful." Unable to come to terms with his own culpability, he confuses her self-defense as a spiteful attempt to emasculate him.

Baldwin further echoes Hurston's perspective on black men and victim status in his rendering of the fallout between Gabriel and Roy. After Gabriel strikes down Elizabeth, Roy comes to her defense, threatening his father with physical violence: "Don't you slap my mother. That's my *mother*. You slap her again, you black bastard, and I swear to God I'll kill you" (48; italics in text). Accustomed to viewing himself as the burden-bearer of the black family, Gabriel has difficulty understanding Roy's stance against him. To his thinking, Roy should be upset with his mother, who, by challenging his authority, provokes him to strike her. Gabriel reveals his bewilderment when he asks, "What did you say?" Roy retorts strongly, "I told you . . . not to touch my mother." Stunned to the point of disbelief, Gabriel replies, "You cursed me." He then ignores Elizabeth's pleas for reconciliation and takes off his belt in preparation to whip Roy. The narrator reports that "[t]ears were in his eyes" (48).

Gabriel expresses intense emotion when whipping Roy because he is genuinely hurt by his son's refusal to support his patriarchal stance. This intense emotion is absent when he strikes Elizabeth because he takes her loyalty for granted, given that she is a woman and his wife. He does not have the same gendered expectations of his son, whom he views as an extension of himself. It is understandable, then, that Gabriel resorts to blaming Elizabeth to court Roy's favor. He thinks that Roy agrees with his twisted patriarchal outlook on the fight and will interpret his blaming Elizabeth as a gesture of support. When he realizes that Roy wants to protect his mother and reject his offering of support, he becomes infuriated to the point of physical violence, viewing Roy's decision as an act of betrayal.

Such wrenching experiences have little impact on Gabriel's distorted perspective on manhood and victimization. He views himself as a victim even in situations in which he clearly possesses the political and social upper hand. His dealings with Esther and Deborah bring the cultural dynamics of this victim status radically into focus. At the time of his extramarital affair with Esther, she holds a reputation in her community as being incorrigible, both for her easy-going ways with men and for the disreputable family to which she belongs. Gabriel, by comparison, enjoys widespread admiration in his community as the most promising of the up-and-coming young ministers in the area. When he reflects back on their illicit relationship, however, he collapses the actual disparities in power, imagining that she, not he, is to blame for their sexual indulgence and the resulting pregnancy.

Baldwin dramatizes the consequences of this victim mind-set by disclosing Gabriel's thoughts on his wife Deborah during the moment when Esther and her mother arrive in church to hear him preach. As Deborah turns to watch them enter the sanctuary, Gabriel begins to make the case to himself for committing adultery. Leering down at his wife from the pulpit, he reflects on "how black and how bony was this wife of his, and how wholly undesirable." He then places his trembling hand on his Bible as Deborah turns to look back at him and he thinks of the "joyless groaning of their marriage bed; and he hated her" (118). When she lies beside him in bed that night he likens her to a "burden laid down at evening which must be picked up once more in the morning" (121). Gabriel's rationale for committing adultery displaces blame for his sexual desire onto Deborah. As a result of her failure to satisfy his sexual appetite, he is forced to seek out sexual gratification in Esther. That he never openly communicates his feelings to Deborah is inconsequential. He expects her to anticipate his feelings of sexual frustration in the same way that she anticipates when he needs his meals prepared and his clothes laundered.

The striking irony here is that Gabriel believes that Deborah benefits from their marriage, especially given that he marries her despite her outcast status as the victim of white gang rape. His description of her as a "burden" that he must "pick up" every morning is revealing. Clearly, he feels that the "honor" of his sacrifice in marriage is not being properly reciprocated in her marital duties. The reality of the situation, however, is that in marrying Deborah, Gabriel acquires a loyal servant who, like his mother, virtually worships the ground upon which he walks. Moreover, he receives the social currency that comes with feeling more righteous than the senior pastors who ridicule Deborah during the great revival. He does not consciously recognize these numerous patriarchal advantages because he has been conditioned to accept them as male entitlements.

Baldwin exposes the effects of this patriarchal conditioning in the way Gabriel imagines himself as a victim in his extramarital affair with Esther. He does so by illuminating the disjuncture between Gabriel's patriarchal claims to victimization and his callous attempt to skirt responsibility for his former lover and unborn child. Baldwin brings this disjuncture sharply into focus by having Gabriel recount his dialogue with Esther following his discovery of her pregnancy. This narrative strategy allows the reader to witness Esther's viewpoint even as Gabriel tries to make the case for her culpability and his innocence. Ultimately, the inclusion of her victim perspective undermines the romanticized self-portrait that Gabriel offers in his reflections, allowing for a realistic account of black women's oppression at the hands of black men.

Gabriel's account of his relationship with Esther is couched within the same patriarchal rhetoric of victimization that he uses to describe his marriage to Deborah. Whereas he blames his wife for his need to pursue sexual gratification outside of marriage, he blames Esther for seducing him into a sexual affair. The most striking example of this victim status is revealed in Gabriel's depiction of his first sexual encounter with Esther. He describes the scene as a spiritual struggle of his will to serve God over hers to corrupt his faith. Ultimately, she triumphs because she is able to capitalize on his sexual frustrations in marriage. He reveals the source of his weakness while staring into Esther's eyes moments before they consummate their relation. He characterizes her "look" of desire as something that "he had not seen for many a long day and night, a look that was never in Deborah's eyes" (126).

Baldwin critiques Gabriel's victim personae by having him recall Esther's protest against having sex in their white employer's kitchen as he tries to undress her. Gabriel remembers "how she protested: 'Not here, not here'" as "his hands tore at her undergarments so that the naked, vivid flesh might meet his hands" (127). Baldwin demonstrates here that Esther never intended to have sex with Gabriel in their white employer's home. Clearly, Gabriel pursues her and orchestrates the seduction. Not only does he shut all the doors and windows to ensure that no one will witness their licentious act, but he also initiates the sex act by placing his hands on Esther's breast and kissing her neck.

Baldwin provides further evidence of Gabriel's distorted perspective of himself as a victim in his conversation with Esther concerning her pregnancy. When Esther proposes that he leave his wife to be with her, he responds as though she is purposely trying to ruin his career as a minister: "How many kinds of a fool you think I am? I got God's work to do—my life don't belong to you. Nor to that baby, neither—if it *is* my baby" (131; italics in text). Offended by his innuendo to skirt responsibility, she returns coldly, "It's your baby . . . and ain't no way in the world to get around that. And it ain't been so very long ago, right here in this *very* room, when looked to me like a life of sin was all you was ready for" (131–32; italics in text). Reemphasizing his feelings of victimization, he replies, "Yes, . . . Satan tempted me and I fell. I ain't the first man been made to fall on account of a wicked woman." Unwilling to accept blame, she returns sharply, "You be careful . . . how you talk to me. I ain't the first girl's been ruined by a holy man, neither" (132).

Gabriel believes that Esther should shoulder the emotional and economic burden of their unborn child because, to his thinking, she is chiefly responsible for initiating the sex. His argument is premised on the notion that he had no control over his own actions—a notion consistent with the victim status upon which his manhood is premised. This notion of powerlessness conveys why he feels no emotional obligations to his unborn child. He views the baby as a product of Esther's deception. To accept responsibility for the child is to acknowledge defeat to her scheme to corrupt his relationship with God.

Although Esther's response to Gabriel's claims to victimization demonstrates her awareness of his intent, her social standing as a promiscuous woman empowers him to treat her with disrespect. She lets him know that she is the true victim in the situation because she is being forced to suffer the consequences of his paternal irresponsibility. As a single black mother she will be stigmatized for life, making it difficult to find a suitable marriage partner, and she will be forced to shoulder the economic and emotional burden of raising a child on her own. To her accusations of being "ruined" by his hands, he responds coldly, "How you going to be ruined? When you been walking through this town just like a harlot, and a-kicking up your heels all over the pasture? How you going to stand there and tell me you been *ruined*? If it hadn't been me, it sure would have been somebody else" (132). His comments show the efficacy of gendered disparities in power. Esther's primary social worth as a woman is bound up in her chastity. Having opted to engage in sexual activity before marriage, she has, in effect, forfeited any claims to social respectability. Her status within this patriarchal system allows Gabriel to feel justified in treating her with disdain even though his past sexual transgressions are comparable to hers, if not far worse.

Esther's desperate attempt to get Gabriel, for whom she has no real affection, to leave his first wife to marry her illustrates the real social conundrum that patriarchy creates for women. As a poor pregnant woman of disreputable social standing, she is virtually at Gabriel's mercy. Her only real political leverage is bound up in her ability to humiliate him publicly by exposing his infidelity. However, even this tactic is limited. If Esther goes public with the news of her pregnancy, the best that she can hope for is Gabriel's public embarrassment—a result that will not necessarily force him to support his child or even guarantee any real harm will be done to his career or marriage. Deborah's supportive response to the knowledge of his infidelity and bastard son provides some gauge as to how the news of Gabriel's relationship would be received publicly.

The disadvantages that public exposure poses to Esther are clear-cut. Given cultural taboos against speaking out publicly against black men of power and prestige, her public airing of their illicit sexual laundry invites the disdain of her entire community (men and women)—a disdain far surpassing that which she currently experiences from her reputation as a promiscuous reprobate. It comes as no surprise, then, that she ultimately agrees to remain silent in exchange for his meager financial assistance. Esther understands that she has more to lose than gain from exposing his hypocrisy. She tells Gabriel, "I would go through this town . . . and tell everybody about the Lord's anointed. Only reason I don't is because I don't want my mamma and daddy to know what a fool I been. I ain't ashamed of *it*—I'm ashamed of *you*—you done made me feel a shame I ain't never felt before. I shamed before my *God*—to let somebody make me cheap, like you done done" (133; italics in text).

Baldwin's contributions to the black male feminist project extend beyond his engagement with black men and patriarchy. He also offers crucial insights into patriarchal complicity for black women. Focusing attention on Elizabeth's and Florence's interior lives, he teases out the cultural factors that encourage black women to support and defend patriarchy. Most importantly, however, he points toward a way out of this complicity, clearing a political pathway for later writers to follow. His strategy plays out thematically in the disparate ways that he represents Elizabeth's and Florence's response to patriarchy. Though both have internalized patriarchal notions of womanhood, Florence manages to recognize elements of her complicity in her relationship to Gabriel and the church. Even as her recognition of complicity does not completely alleviate her investments in patriarchy, it does equip her with enough confidence to confront her brother about his abusive treatment of women. Elizabeth never rises to this level of awareness. She becomes preoccupied with the patriarchal expectations of black women's self-sacrifice to the point that she begins to shoulder the emotional burden of black male suffering. She even blames herself for allowing Richard, her former lover, to commit suicide.

Baldwin dramatizes the process of Elizabeth's complicity when she agonizes in her altar reflections over the mistakes that she has made in her life. He does so by illuminating Elizabeth's complex relationship with her aunt—a relationship that deeply informs her self-deprecating ideas about womanhood, religion, and men and reveals the tenacious complicity whereby women police each other into accepting patriarchal paradigms of womanhood. Instead of being supportive of Elizabeth following the death of her mother, her aunt tries to lower her self-esteem so that she will embrace her subordinate gender status. Her primary method of policing is to threaten Elizabeth that her prideful attitude will provoke God's wrath against her: "You little miss great-I-am . . . you better watch your step, you hear me? You go walking around with your nose in the air, the Lord's going to let you fall right down to the bottom of the ground. *You* mark my words. You'll *see*" (156; italics in text).

The significance of these warnings/threats to Elizabeth's understanding of womanhood become evident in the ways she negotiates her feelings for her deceived lover Richard, the kind of man her aunt warned her against. Part of Elizabeth's spiritual crisis is that she cannot force herself to regret her relationship with him, and this makes her feel that she is inviting God's wrath. This mind-set stems from being taught by her aunt that God functions as a type of gender policeman who will punish sexually deviant women until they fully repent of their sins. Elizabeth feels ultimately deserving of punishment because she conflates patriarchal expectations of gender roles with religious doctrine. Reflecting on this emotional dilemma at the altar, she notes that "[n]ot even tonight, in the heart's nearly impenetrable secret place, where the truth is hidden and where only truth can live, could she wish that she had not known him; or deny that, so long as he was there, the rejoicing of Heaven could have meant nothing to her—that, being forced to choose between Richard and God, she could only, even with weeping, have turned away from God" (157).

Here she rebels against the patriarchal expectations of gender roles bound up in her ideas about God. Her emotional choice of Richard over God is in effect a choice to denounce the gender mandates of patriarchy. Metaphorically speaking, Richard ultimately wins out over God in Elizabeth's mind because as an atheist he provides her with a viable alternative to subordinate gender status. The most redeeming aspect of his thinking for Elizabeth is that he does not consider her less desirable as a potential spouse because she has sex with him prior to marriage. Moreover, he does not hold her to a higher moral and ethical standard because she is a woman.

Elizabeth acknowledges the empowering impact of Richard's egalitarian ideas indirectly when she relays her feelings about his use of profanity. She notes that "he never 'watched' his language with her, which at first she took as evidence of his contempt because she had fallen so easily, and which she later took as evidence of his love" (165). Her change in attitude derives largely from the realization that his refusal to "watch" his language in front of her is a sign that gender does not ultimately govern the way that he evaluates her morality. That is, he does not use profanity in front of her because he thinks that she is morally corrupt but because he views her as his gender equal. Once Elizabeth intuits his egalitarian motive she is no longer offended by his use of profanity because she understands its political significance.

The liberating aspects of her relationship with Richard, however, are not enough to offset her internalized notions of gendered expectations, particularly the notion that as a woman she must prioritize the emotional and material needs of "her man" over herself. Her response to Richard's suicide reveals her deep investment in patriarchy. When she recalls the events that led up to his death, she ponders ways that she could have protected him, wondering whether her choice to conceal her pregnancy contributed to his suicide. Her initial choice of silence stemmed from a desire not to add to his already stressful circumstances. In retrospect, however, she feels that the news of her pregnancy might have provided Richard with a purpose to live. For this reason, Elizabeth agonizes that perhaps "she had lost her love because she had not, in the end, believed in it enough" (168).

Elizabeth does not consider other factors because she views Richard and black men as powerless victims of white oppression. Her propensity for self-blame underscores the extent of her investment in black patriarchy. She feels that she failed in her duties as a black woman because she was unable to nurture him back into health. Her guilt, then, extends beyond feeling responsible for his death. She feels culturally inadequate as a black woman because she could not take care of her man.

Florence also experiences similar feelings of inadequacy and guilt. Afflicted with a cancer for which she can find no medical explanation or cure, she begins to wonder if her mysterious illness is God's way of punishing her for challenging patriarchy. Her fears escalate to the point that she returns to the church in search of redemption. Ultimately, she hopes that making peace with God will put an end to her physical suffering and bring much-needed closure to her strained relationships with friends and family.

Hers is a dilemma that is significantly different from Elizabeth's, however. Having so deeply internalized the expectation of black female self-sacrifice, Elizabeth accepts responsibility for her own victimization at the hands of black men. Unlike Elizabeth, Florence is acutely aware of the victim status that allows black men, like her brother Gabriel, to garner admiration and sympathy in the black community even as they openly exploit black women. She is also aware of the ways that black women, like her mother Rachel, become policing agents in maintaining these patriarchal patterns.

Baldwin shows that Florence's knowledge alone is not enough to resist the cultural pressures to embrace black patriarchy. What she sorely lacks is the additional support of a community. The only community that can provide such support is the black church—an institution that typically views gender issues from the dominant male perspective. Her support network is itself a primary source of the problem, entangling her in a gendered double-consciousness. To borrow W. E. B. Du Bois's phrasing, she finds herself trapped in "a world which yields [her] no true self-consciousness, but only lets [her] see [her]self through the revelation" of the black male Other (*Souls of Black Folks* 2). Her chief dilemma is that she does not have a true support network to authenticate her gender-specific experiences of oppression. As such, she is always at war within herself, championing the cause of black women's empowerment even as she seeks acceptance from a patriarchal institution of power.

This mental tug-of-war plays out in her return to the church. In a dramatic act of humility, she begins to sing a song of tribute to her deceased mother—a woman so deeply invested in patriarchy that she deprived her daughter of material and emotional resources to ensure the well-being of her son Gabriel. Her tribute suggests that she is prepared to forgive her mother and move beyond the conflicts that drove them apart in life. She cannot keep her focus on her mother and healing, however, because Gabriel begins to gloat inwardly over her public display of suffering. His gloating infuriates her because she understands that he views her downfall as a patriarchal victory. The narrator reports that she "knew that Gabriel rejoiced, not that her humility might lead her to grace, but only that some private anguish had brought her low: her song revealed that she was suffering and this her brother was glad to see" (65). Florence's initial response is to abandon her desire for reinstatement to the church: "For a moment her pride stood up; the resolution that had brought her to this place tonight faltered, and she felt that if Gabriel was the Lord's anointed, she would rather die and endure Hell for all eternity than bow before His altar" (66). However, she "strangles her pride" and rises with the rest of the congregation to continue in praise and worship.

The altar scene demonstrates that Florence does not want to become an accomplice in the maintenance of black patriarchy. She is aware, on a conscious level, that by returning to the church she is indirectly confirming Gabriel's patriarchal authority. This awareness explains her initial reaction, when she decides that going to hell (read: abandoning her communal support network) would be preferable to bowing before Gabriel's altar of patriarchal power. She changes her mind, however, and decides not to confront Gabriel because she experiences her refusal to capitulate to his patriarchal authority as a sinful act of pride. Her decision is informed largely by her cultural investment in the church. Reared to believe that complete humility is the only path to spiritual salvation, Florence feels that her rejection of Gabriel could jeopardize her relationship with God. She is thrown into a moral and political crisis, then, because even though she does not want to acquiesce to the patriarchal authority embodied in her brother, she also does not want her pride to prevent her from receiving spiritual salvation and the support of the church.

Florence evaluates her options within the rules of a patriarchal institution. When she restrains herself from confronting Gabriel, she thinks of what she is doing as resisting him and protecting her spiritual process. The problem with her rationale is that her "choices" are circumscribed within the cultural framework of black patriarchy. As long as she operates within this framework, she cannot navigate her way out of complicity. In effect, she becomes complicit in her own subjugation despite her efforts to combat patriarchy.

It would be a mistake to view Florence's situation as hopeless. Baldwin depicts her gendered double-consciousness to underscore the cultural obstacles that need to be addressed in order to promote real social change in the black community. Florence undergoes a necessary stage of political evolution—she begins to scrutinize the patriarchal standards upon which she bases her womanhood. Though she never fully completes this political evolution within the scope of the narrative, Baldwin shows that she never abandons her skepticism about patriarchy. Note, for instance, the way that she evaluates her relationship to her mother while she kneels before the altar. Given that she harbors deep regrets for having left her mother on her deathbed to pursue her own dreams of prosperity, the reader anticipates that she will take on the blame for having severed the relationship. When she recounts the events that led up to her exodus, however, she does not envision herself as an irresponsible daughter. Rather she rightly assesses that her mother is a policing agent of black patriarchy who seeks to shame her into gender compliance. Florence notes that her mother was "content to stay in this cabin and do washing for the white folks, though she was old and her back was sore. And she wanted Florence, also, to be content—helping with the washing, and fixing meals and keeping Gabriel quiet" (72). She understands that her mother made these sacrifices—and expected her to make them as well—to ensure that Gabriel is adequately nurtured as a "manchild." She also understands that her mother is so deeply invested in black patriarchy that she views her favoritism as responsible parenting and Florence's decision to leave as a selfish act.

That Florence does not trivialize her relationship with her mother or her reasons for leaving is crucial, especially given the circumstances that have led her back to the church. Her need for a community has not blinded her to the realities of black patriarchy and complicity. In this way, she has progressed politically far beyond Elizabeth and Deborah because she recognizes that her experiences of patriarchal abuse are legitimate even though she harbors feelings of guilt for having tried to resist complicity.

Baldwin dramatizes this political progression in Florence's final thoughts at the altar. After she reflects on her lifelong struggles with patriarchy, she experiences a mixture of terror and rage concerning her circumstances—terror because she feels that God will end her life and condemn her to hell because she tried to resist complicity, and rage at God because she feels that she is being unjustly condemned. The narrator reports that she was "divided between a terrible longing to surrender [to God] and a desire to call God into account. Why had he preferred her mother and her brother, the old, black woman, and the low, black man, while she, who had sought only to walk upright, was come to die, alone and in poverty, in a dirty, furnished room? She beat her fists heavily against the altar. He [Gabriel] . . . would live, and, smiling, watch her go down into the grave! And her mother would be there, leaning over the gates of Heaven, to see her daughter burning in the pit" (90).

Notably, Florence does not assume a self-sacrificial posture when evaluating her circumstances. Rather than dismiss the cultural factors that governed her social reality and blindly accept culpability for own victimization, she becomes infuriated with God—the metaphorical embodiment of black patriarchal power—and begins to question his authority and fairness. She is especially distraught over the prospect that her brother, who has spent a lifetime victimizing black women, and her mother, who tried to police her into a self-sacrificial gender role, will be rewarded with eternal salvation while she, the victim of black patriarchy, will be condemned to eternal damnation. The question that she poses to herself concerning the matter is clearly rhetorical. She believes that God wrongly favors the victimizers over the victimized. Gabriel and her mother are direct and indirect proponents of a patriarchal system that subjugates black women, and yet God allows them to prosper both materially and spiritually. In stark contrast, she—a victim of this patriarchal system and a champion for other women who have suffered under it—becomes a candidate for God's wrath, incurring both physical and material hardships.

Here Florence begins to revise the self-sacrificial gender models of cultural understanding. Her need for a community explains her ambivalent desire to "surrender" to God on the one hand and call him "into account" on the other. Even as her fear of isolation prevents her from completely severing ties with God and the church, she rightly directs her frustration and anger toward God rather than herself. That she is even able to entertain the possibility that God has wrongly condemned her and black women for combating patriarchy demonstrates that she is moving toward a more cogent and useful understanding of complicity, despite her desire for cultural acceptance and support.

Baldwin demonstrates the political significance of Florence's new insights by having her lend support to John (the only male in the novel who empathizes with black women's suffering) after his father Gabriel tries to discount his spiritual experience on the threshing floor. Her support is crucial to John because he needs someone to validate his spiritual experience—an experience that radically alters his romanticized image of his stepfather, revealing him to be an abusive man who uses his patriarchal authority to dominate and control his wife and children. In direct opposition to Gabriel's expressed doubts about John's spiritual conversion—"I want to see you live it. It's more than a notion" (207)—Florence encourages him "to fight the good fight" against evil influence. Moreover, she counsels, "Don't you get weary, and don't you get scared. Because I *know* the Lord's done laid His hands on you" (208; italics in text).

By reassuring John that his spiritual conversion is real and important to God, Florence directly undermines Gabriel's patriarchal authority and offers John a viable alternative to patriarchal communities and belief systems. At base, she confirms that his father does not have the power to define or judge his spiritual reality. She accomplishes this by asserting her own gendered authority as a witness of God. By asserting that she "knows" God has confirmed John's conversion, Florence demonstrates that her version of Christianity does not need to be authenticated by Gabriel or the black church. Her assertion shows John that he can build a community with her that is not ultimately governed by patriarchy. Little wonder, then, that John responds with tears and jubilation,

"Yes . . . yes, I'm going to serve the Lord" (208). He recognizes the liberating power of his aunt's advice and insights.

The most salient evidence of Florence's political progress is her confrontation with Gabriel. Notably, Baldwin structures the confrontation so that it occurs after she counsels John, allowing the reader to witness her advice to John put into action. From a thematic standpoint, Baldwin uses this confrontation to introduce a possible path beyond patriarchal complicity. Florence provides a guidepost for this path when she calls attention to the victim status that allows Gabriel and black men to erase their subjugation of black women. She brings this phenomenon of erasure to the fore when she takes Gabriel to task for his abandonment of Esther and his first son Royal, a situation that he hides from public view even though he believes it has no bearing on his moral character. Florence exposes Gabriel's patriarchal blind spots in a heated debate over death and salvation that occurs on their walk home from evening church service. Convinced of his own moral preparedness, Gabriel offers his sister an indirect warning: "I pray . . . it [the death angel] finds you ready [for Judgment Day] sister." When she redirects the warning to him, asking if he will be ready for Judgment Day, he replies confidently, "I know my name is written in the Book of Life . . . [and] I know I'm going to look on my Saviour's face in glory." She returns, "Yes, . . . we's all going to be together there. Mama, and you, and me, and Deborah—and what was the name of that little girl who died not long after I left home?" Oblivious at this point to whom she refers, he retorts, "What little girl who died? . . . A *lot* of folks died after *you* left home—you left your *mother* on her dying bed." Ignoring his verbal jab, she returns, "This girl was a mother, too . . . Look like she went North all by herself, and had her baby, and died—weren't nobody to help her. Deborah wrote me about it. Sure, you ain't forgotten that girl's name, Gabriel!" Awakened to her knowledge of Esther and Royal, he responds with stunned silence. Florence then asserts, "You ain't forgotten her name . . . You can't tell me you done forgot her name. Is you going to look on her face, too? Is her name written in the Book of Life?" (211).

Florence clearly understands why Gabriel inserts their mother into the verbal sparring. He wants to shame her into silence and assert his moral superiority. She shirked her womanly obligations to her sick and dying mother to pursue prosperity in the North, while he stayed behind to care for their mother alone. Her failure within patriarchy as a daughter and caregiver is tantamount to religious blasphemy. Rather than accept Gabriel's indictment, Florence strikes back. In doing so, she sends a clear message that he can no longer bully her with his twisted patriarchal standards. Her bold stance against Gabriel completely alters the political terms of the debate, forcing him to justify the rationale that he uses to indict her and absolve himself. Accustomed to Florence and black women accepting patriarchy, Gabriel loses a critical advantage. He cannot openly play on sympathy as the chief victim of racial oppression or as the burden-bearer of the black family. What he does instead is couch his victim status in religious rhetoric. He cannot be held accountable for abandoning Esther and Roy because God has forgiven him. To judge him as immoral is to undermine God's authority, not his. "I done answered . . . already before my God," he tells Florence. "I ain't got to answer now, in front of you" (212).

Florence recognizes Gabriel's power play. To avoid having to own up to his sins against black women, he invokes the ultimate patriarch in God as his final judge and juror. To counter this power play Florence introduces Deborah's letter to show Gabriel that even if God has forgiven him, his many victims have not. The letter bears witness to Deborah's bitterness toward him for having to endure his lies and deceit. More importantly, it breaks the collective gendered silence that emboldens him to displace his moral failings onto black women and skirt responsibility for his abusive behavior. The letter unnerves Gabriel because he has never had to grapple with women's feelings. Nor has he had to account for the patriarchal privilege that allows him to ignore their suffering. His initial reaction to the letter reveals his bewilderment: "He recognized Deborah's uncertain, trembling hand, and he could see her again in the cabin, bending over the table, laboriously trusting to paper the bitterness she had not spoken. It had lived in her silence, then, all of those years? He could not believe it. She had been praying for him as she died—she had sworn to meet him in glory. And yet, this letter, her witness, spoke, breaking her long silence, now that she was beyond his reach forever" (212).

Given the egregious nature of Gabriel's betrayal of Deborah—impregnating another woman and then stealing money from his wife to cover it up—it would seem that her bitterness toward him should not come as a surprise. It does surprise him, however, because Deborah never openly expressed any anger or resentment toward him. Gabriel did not entertain the idea that she masked her true feelings because he expects women to cater to him. Thus he took it for granted that Deborah's silence represented her forgiveness. In effect, she becomes a cipher for his own patriarchal beliefs about black women and personal responsibility. Her silence confirms for him that he is still a "good man" despite his sins against her and the church (he does not feel that he has sinned against Esther). This patriarchal mind-set explains why he derives consolation from replacing the money he steals from Deborah. Doing so allows him to feel like he is acting responsibly even though publicly he never has to contend with wrecking the lives of two women.

Gabriel fears Deborah's letter because it breaks the complicity of silence that allows him to dominate women with impunity. His fear becomes apparent in the way that he reacts to her deception. Rather than express feelings of responsibility or guilt for having generated his wife's bitterness toward him, he responds as if she betrayed him by masking her feelings of bitterness in expressions of loyalty. Her betrayal is exacerbated by the fact that she is dead and "beyond his reach forever" (212), leaving him powerless to refute her feelings. What becomes clear is that he relies heavily upon black women's complicity to confirm his patriarchal authority. Without this complicity, he loses much of his ability to dominate and control women, which is why the letter presents a threat to him beyond what it reveals about his undisclosed affair with Esther. It upsets his own illusions about his manhood by forcing him to contend with his lack of control over Deborah.

Florence's confrontation with him reveals that, even though she fears cultural ostracism, she does not allow the church or Gabriel to pressure her into silence. Rather she tries to use her limited power to make her protest heard and to break her brother's hold over his wife and children. Specifically, she uses Deborah's letter as a bargaining chip to pressure him to stop abusing his family. If he does not radically alter his abuse, she plans to use the letter to incriminate him in the eyes of his wife and the church.

Her strategy runs many of the same risks as Esther's. She has no guarantee that exposing Gabriel as an adulterer will diminish his dominance at home or in the church. Given cultural taboos against maligning black men in the public sphere, her strategy could easily backfire. Elizabeth and the church could side with Gabriel and label her an emasculator. So, the critical question emerges: What is going to prevent Florence from succumbing to the same pressures that effectively silenced Esther? General consensus among scholars is that Baldwin resists closure in *Go Tell It*. He does not provide clear-cut answers to whether John will cave in to his father's distorted perspective on women, religion, manhood, and sexuality or whether he will chart a new course for himself. What is clear is that John is more optimistic about his chances of success because of the encouragement he receives from Florence and Elisha. But the reader does not know whether Florence's strategy of coercion will be enough to pressure her brother to end his patriarchal abuse toward his wife and children. At question also is whether she will survive her cancer long enough to follow through on her threat in the event that Gabriel refuses to change.

Despite these uncertainties, there are many promising signs that Florence will succeed. Working in her favor is that she seeks out a new community in John as his mentor. Following his "conversion" on the threshing floor she provides him with the encouragement he needs to validate his conversion. Most importantly, she offers him an alternative model to patriarchy that may allow him to break free from his father's influence. The payoff is that in mentoring John she can find someone to appreciate her feminist perspective and empathize with her fight against patriarchy. In this way, she can avoid the threat of cultural alienation that silences Esther.

Another promising sign is Florence's dogged refusal to give in to Gabriel's authority even in times of crisis. Her willpower becomes evident during her stint at the altar. Overwhelmed with guilt, she concludes that her pride is the primary reason that God is punishing her with illness. Given her desire to reconcile with God and to put an end to her physical suffering, it would seem that she would relinquish her fight with Gabriel. Instead, she becomes more adamant about ending his reign of abuse, presenting him with an incriminating letter from Deborah that she has held in her possession for more than a decade. Thus, despite the bouts of guilt and fear she experiences at the altar, she does not abandon her campaign against Gabriel and patriarchal abuse.

She articulates her resolve in the warning she gives him before they depart for the night. "When I go, brother," she asserts, "you better tremble, cause I ain't going to go in silence" (215). Her warning shows the reader that she has cleared a crucial hurdle regarding complicity. Rather than cave in to the pressures to remain silent, she bears witness to patriarchal abuse in the black community. Even if her strategy against Gabriel does ultimately backfire (in the event that he ignores her warning and she follows through with her plans to expose him), she will have initiated an important first step toward dismantling black patriarchal regimes.

Even as Baldwin stops short of having Florence and black women emerge completely from under the stronghold of patriarchy, he provides a useful model for how they can begin the process of resistance. Specifically, he demonstrates the level of personal risk and sacrifice required to promote real social change for women in the black community. Florence is able to confront her brother and patriarchy only because she desires social justice for black women more than she fears cultural alienation. Despite the high social risks involved, she feels at once compelled and obligated as a woman to come to Elizabeth's aid. The message that Baldwin conveys through her decision is that even seemingly moderate challenges to patriarchy can render significant results. Had Florence remained silent she would have given Gabriel free rein to oppress his wife specifically and black women in general. By standing up to him, she has at least placed him on notice that his abusive behavior will not continue to go unquestioned. Even though her stance against Gabriel will probably not have a significant impact on dismantling the male-focused infrastructure of the black church, it can, and most likely will, have a redeeming and lasting impact on the lives of Elizabeth and black women. If but for this reason alone, she will have made a necessary and important contribution to ending male dominance in the black community.

Thematically speaking, Baldwin makes significant contributions to the black male feminist project by defining the problems of black patriarchy across gender lines. He demonstrates that even men who experience tremendous racial oppression are capable of victimizing others. Dominating black women becomes a way for them to feel empowered in a world that denies them full access to the (white) trappings of manhood. Baldwin shows that such thinking is difficult to explode because black women participate unknowingly in defending and policing black patriarchy. Further compounding the problem is that women like Florence who have the desire to resist complicity must overcome intense feelings of guilt and the threat of cultural alienation. Even if they manage to overcome these obstacles, they require the additional support of a community to sustain them against the constant pressure to embrace patriarchy. By leaving Florence's fate open to question, Baldwin charges the reader to decide the outcome. One could interpret this literary move as a call to political action. Black women like Florence can succeed only if blacks across gender lines are willing to come to their aid. Those that heed the call can expect the path toward dismantling black patriarchy to be long and taxing. But they can also find a role model in Florence, illustrating that open resistance to patriarchy is productive and necessary. What Baldwin ultimately demonstrates in *Go Tell It on the Mountain* is that ending patriarchal rule in the black community will require more than getting black men to recognize the problems of their victim status and to change their abusive behavior toward black women. It will also require that black women become more aware of how they support and police patriarchy in their behavior toward men and each other. Resistant strategies that do not take all of these complex factors into account are doomed to fail.

3

"KILLING THE WHITE GIRL FIRST"
Understanding the Politics of Black Manhood in Toni Morrison's *Paradise*

THE POLITICAL ISSUES CONCERNING black masculinity that Toni Morrison engages in *Paradise* (1998) are certainly not new in her work. Both *Song of Solomon* (1977) and *Beloved* (1987) illuminate the pernicious effects of patriarchal thinking by revealing the extent to which black men exploit their gender privilege over black women. Foregrounding the socioeconomic factors that compel black men to abuse black women, the novels focus primarily on the immediate impact of black patriarchal thinking rather than on its sociopolitical origins. In *Paradise,* however, Morrison probes the sociopolitical origins of black patriarchal thinking to address the psychological and emotional effects of slavery on black men. Most crucially, she notes that slavery decimated black men's cultural self-consciousness by divesting them of their African languages, histories, and religions. As a result, they rely upon white male ideologies to establish their concept of manhood. By underscoring this psychosocial dynamic, Morrison calls attention to the unique complications that confront black men when they try to establish a viable model of manhood in a self-segregated black community.

To ground her argument historically, Morrison invokes the Booker T. Washington–W. E. B. Du Bois debate regarding the proper course for black social uplift. In her story about an all-black Oklahoma town during the post–World War II era, she calls attention to the problematics of the Ruby men's patriarchal ethos by showing how Deacon (Deek) and Steward Morgan attempt to address the Du Boisian problem of double consciousness by employing conservative Washingtonian politics, informed by white supremacist ideologies. Morrison contrasts the brothers with Reverend Richard Misner, a black nationalist minister, and Connie (Consolata), the de facto leader of the Convent women, both of whom undergo spiritual transformations that give them insight into the central importance of gender dynamics in the construction of double consciousness. The key for both is rejecting the unstated premises of the white supremacist (Washingtonian) world in which they live. Connie recovers the African-Brazilian name and culture that were stripped from her by her Catholic education; the recovery allows her to become the spiritual and cultural advisor for the other Convent women. Misner—who is already half-conscious of the extent to which slavery conditioned blacks to internalize white supremacy—undergoes a spiritual transformation that makes him aware of not only the destructive patriarchal (Washingtonian) perspective of the Ruby men but of the patriarchal underpinnings of his own black nationalistic perspective. Like Connie, Misner serves as a cultural mediator for his community. His task is to help the Ruby men understand how their internalization of white gender and cultural norms has distorted their view of black women, African culture, and themselves. While Morrison's political message is ultimately hopeful, she clearly understands the difficulties of addressing patriarchy in the black community; only one of the nine Ruby leaders who storm the Convent seeks out Misner for spiritual counseling.

A summary of Morrison's most complex plot to date underscores the difficulty of effecting a real transformation in the attitudes concerning black patriarchy in the black community. *Paradise* traces the interconnected lives and histories of the 8-rock (dark-skinned) citizens of Ruby and the five women living in the convent several miles outside the town. Ruby is named in honor of Deek and Steward's sister, Ruby, who died, shortly after the town was established, because the closest hospital, ninety miles away, refused to admit black patients. The brothers establish the town to preserve the legacy of their grandfather, Zechariah (Coffee, Big Papa) Morgan, who in 1889 founded an all-black town in Oklahoma called Haven. When the twins leave in 1942 to fight in the war, Haven is thriving; when they return home seven years later, they find the town on the verge of social and economic collapse. As a result, they assemble the original founding families of Haven, pack up the Oven that was erected by the Old Fathers to commemorate their tumultuous journey from the South to Oklahoma, and establish a new town 240 miles to the west. For more than two decades Ruby experiences relative social and economic success. However, in the early 1970s, during the height of the Black Power movement, the strict social codes that the New Fathers of Ruby establish to keep unwanted visitors from living in this town turn the younger generation against them. Under the spiritual guidance of Reverend Misner, the teenagers begin to challenge the traditions, lore, and elitist politics of the New Fathers. In 1976, after a politically charged wedding between the Morgan and Fleetwood clans fails to ameliorate the burgeoning social discord in the town, Deek and Steward begin to worry that Ruby will succumb to the same fate as Haven.

Unable to come to terms with their responsibility for the town's social demise, the brothers scapegoat five socially outcast women who reside in a former convent on the outskirts of town. They rally seven other men—all of whom are looking for ways to explain (away) personal, social, and economic "failures"—and raid the convent. During the raid Deek reencounters his ex-lover, Connie, whom he hasn't seen since their adulterous affair more than twenty years earlier. When she says, "You're back," Deek at first believes that she is addressing him but soon recognizes she is looking past him at someone he cannot see. Before he can ask Connie what she sees, his twin brother shoots her in the head.

Steward's act of cruelty forges an emotional wedge between the brothers, but also sparks an arduous process of reconsidering the meaning of Ruby's (and Haven's) patriarchal ethos. Breaking with his tradition of only confiding in his brother, Deek takes Misner into his confidence and begins to understand the implications of Ruby's rhetoric of "protecting the female." Ultimately, this requires him to come to terms with the trauma of his slave ancestry and the historical legacy of Haven. While Morrison portrays this as a necessary step, Deek's personal growth does not necessarily herald the end of patriarchy in Ruby. Steward feels vindicated by his actions, and by the novel's end he begins to groom his nephew, K. D., to be the next leader of the Ruby patriarchy.

To date, reviewers and critics of *Paradise* have given surprisingly little attention to Morrison's interrogation of black masculinity. The most insightful studies focus instead on the politics of separatism that undergirds the novel. Missy Dehn Kubitschek, for example, argues that *Paradise* "investigates the divergence between the social realities of a separatist establishment and an all-black Utopia." While Morrison is sympathetic to "the origins of separatism," Kubitschek writes, she "depicts it as ultimately destructive of the community that it is designed to protect" (180). Deek and Steward's fundamental problem, according to Kubitschek, is that they "see the world through . . . [binary] oppositions [of] good versus bad, themselves versus the young hooligans, good young girls like Arnette versus bad ones like Billie Delia, [and] Ruby versus the convent." Ultimately, Kubitschek concludes, "*Paradise* shows that opposed, mutually exclusive categories can never be maintained because they deny social complexity" (180).

Like Kubitschek, J. Brooks Bouson argues that Morrison's project is to reveal the bankruptcy of separatist politics. When the Old Fathers founded Haven, Bouson observes, "they removed themselves from the larger society with its shaming categories of difference only to forge their own system of inclusion and exclusion which they pass down to their Ruby descendants" (200). Unlike Kubitschek, Bouson emphasizes the ideological dynamic that compels the 8-rock men to displace their shame onto lighter-skinned black men. She argues that the "Disallowing"—the defining moment in Haven lore where Zechariah's crew are turned away from the all-black town in Fairly, Oklahoma, because of intraracial color prejudice—sheds light on the self-effacing ideology of the Ruby men. According to Bouson, the secret pleasure that Deek and Steward take in the failure of other all-black towns founded by ex-slaves "points to their reactive desire to turn the tables on and witness the humiliation of their black humiliators" (199). She argues that the twins' displaced bitterness and separatist politics are the "result of and reaction to the self-loathing that grows out of internalized racism" (199).

While these essays identify important rhetorical patterns in *Paradise,* neither specifically addresses Morrison's critique of white supremacist ideology as it relates to the construction of black manhood. Nor do they engage the interracial power dynamics between white men and black men which foster intraracial hostility among lighter- and darker-skinned black men. Bouson argues that "self-loathing" and "internalized racism" bolster Deek and Steward's desire to humiliate their black humiliators, but her argument reproduces a conventional discourse on black masculinity that links black-on-black (male) violence to pathologies of self-hate. Such arguments, I contend, obscure the "pathology" of self-aggrandizement or racial superiority by focusing attention on the psychosocial symptoms of white supremacy, i.e., black-on-black crime, rather than the historical derivation of the ideology itself. Morrison makes it clear that the Ruby men take special pride in their coal-black (8-rock) skin. Like Marcus Garvey's "Back to Africa" movement in the 1920s and adherents to the black power movement, the Ruby men invert the ideology of white supremacy to underscore the superiority of black men. Thus it is the Ruby men's racial *superiority* complex—inextricably and ironically grounded in white supremacist notions of patriarchy—that is under scrutiny in *Paradise.*

Given the well-established significance of Morrison's opening lines, it is important to understand how the first sentences of *Paradise*—easily her most provocative opening to date—fits into her interrogation of black masculinity. The novel opens, "They shoot the white girl first. With the rest they can take their time"(1).

"They" are the nine Ruby leaders: Deek and Steward Morgan, Wisdom Poole, Sargeant Person, K. D., Arnold and Jeff Fleetwood (father and son), and Harper and Menus Jury (father and son). Morrison conceals the men's identities until the end of the novel when Lone DuPres retells the story of the raid on the Convent. Even then, the reader cannot be certain who is speaking in the opening chapter. Morrison's narrative strategy foregrounds the black masculine politics that inform the town leaders' social, cultural, religious, and economic politics. By deferring identification of the nine men, Morrison calls attention to the shared patriarchal consciousness of the group, a consciousness that allows them to justify murdering the convent women under the guise of protecting the moral integrity of the Ruby women.

Morrison invokes the black man–white woman murder taboo in her opening lines to underscore the extent to which the Ruby men's idea of "true" manhood is informed by their internalized white supremacist notions of masculinity. To appreciate its place in Morrison's political strategy, it is necessary to contextualize the taboo historically. For more than half a century after the failure of Reconstruction, hundreds of black men were lynched in the South by white men who almost always claimed to be defending white female virtue. Seeking to regain complete social and economic control over blacks, white conservatives orchestrated a campaign of terrorism whereby they played upon white fears that social equality in the South would give black men license to rape white women. Unchallenged notions of black primitivism legitimized such beliefs and provided white southerners with a discourse in which "protecting white womanhood" justified violence against black men. In "Murder, Memory, and the Flight of the Incubus" Glenda Gilmore rightly observes that "patriarchy's allure to white men lay not in its duties [to white women], but in . . . the power that the heights of social hierarchy conferred upon white men. That power gave them control over white women, over white children, and over black people of all ages and both sexes" (82).

The relationship between black men and white women was

circumscribed by this white male supremacist discourse. Socially, economically, and in some instances physically emasculated, many black men felt that to possess and control white female bodies was to co-opt white patriarchal dominance, and to attain "true" manhood. As Devon W. Carbado insightfully notes in "The Construction of O.J. as a Racial Victim," "Slavery prevented Black men from 'controlling' Black women's sexuality in the way that white men controlled white women's and Black women's sexuality. And since 'slavery coexisted with male dominance in the wider society, *Black men as men* constituted a potential threat to the establishment order of white supremacy.' Thus, the law denied Black men the patriarchal privilege that white men enjoyed; Black men could not prevent white men from raping or otherwise abusing their wives, their sisters and their daughters. They were denied the 'right' to be *men;* they were 'emasculated'" (170).

For the nine Ruby men, then, to kill the white woman is the ultimate act of black male liberation, a means of dismantling the white supremacist regime that has historically emasculated them. This dynamic is underscored in Lone's retelling of the raid on the Convent. After Steward shoots the white woman with "sensual appraising eyes," the narrator informs the reader that the men, "fondling their weapons" as they step over the white woman's wounded body, enter the Convent. Her death made them feel "suddenly so young and good." It "reminded [them] that guns are more than decoration, intimidation or comfort. They are meant" (285). The revealing sexual language used to describe the shooting of the white girl invokes images of sexual assault. Given that white patriarchal power is inextricably linked to the domination of both (white and black) female and black male bodies, to "rape" the white girl, for the Ruby men, is to turn white patriarchy on its head. They reclaim control of their own bodies by gaining access to and control over the coveted entitlement of white patriarchy—namely, white female bodies.

Morrison's play on the syntax in describing this scene underscores the notion of black masculinity as an *act* of sexual domination and meaning-making. In the sentence "They are meant," Morrison represents the past tense verb "meant" as at once a verb and a noun, the predicate nominative of the sentence. By doing so she reveals that the murder of the white woman is self-valorizing for the men. They fondle their phallic guns as they step over the conquered white female body because they are aroused by what they perceive as the ultimate act of black male liberation. The men can "take their time" killing the black women because, to a large degree, they already have access to, if not control over, black female bodies. Whether or not the white woman is "white" in accordance with the Jim Crow-inspired "One-Drop Rule" is irrelevant in this instance. Most important is that the men *perceive* the woman as white.

It is also worth noting that the order in which the women are killed is purely circumstantial. No effort is made by any of the men to kill the white woman first. But by framing the killings as if they are meticulously calculated, Morrison demonstrates the extent to which written history is re-presented and constructed in a way that legitimates a white supremacist and patriarchal narrative.

Morrison invokes the interracial taboo at the outset of the novel to illuminate the ways that the Ruby men—themselves victims of white patriarchy—utilize a similar rationale to justify their slaying of the unarmed Convent women. This mode of thinking is based on the belief that women need to be protected and that their social worth inheres in their conventional roles as mothers, wives, and daughters. The nine men demonize the Convent women and call specific attention to their unwomanly behavior. While scanning "dusty mason jars" and canned goods, the men notice that the women are behind schedule on canning vegetables for the winter. "Slack," one man thinks. "August just around the corner and these women have not even sorted, let alone washed, the jars" (4). Misidentifying the healing practices of the convent women as satanic, an unidentified member of the Ruby men reflects, "How can their plain brains think up such things: revolting sex, deceit and the sly torture of children? Out here in wide-open space tucked away in a mansion—no one to bother or insult them—they managed to call into question the *value* of almost every woman he knew" (8; my italics). The revealing patriarchal language illuminates the real threat that the women pose to the nine Ruby men. The women's tacit refusal to conform to prescribed gender roles threatens to collapse the political apparatus that grants the men social control over the women. To challenge the viability of gender prescriptions *is* to question the authority of the men who created them.

Shortly after he condemns the Convent women, the unidentified narrator delineates a patriarchal narrative highlighting the safety that Ruby provides for "virtuous" 8-rock women. "Certainly," the man thinks, "there wasn't a slack or sloven woman anywhere in town and the reasons, he thought, were clear. From the beginning its people were free and protected. A sleepless woman could always rise from her bed, wrap a shawl around her shoulders, and sit on the steps in the moonlight. And if she felt like it she could walk out the yard and on down the road. No lamp and no fear. A hiss-crackle from the side of the road would never scare her because whatever it was that made the sound, it wasn't something creeping up on her. *Nothing for ninety miles around thought she was prey*" (8; my italics). The man imagines that this sleepless woman is reflecting on her womanly duties as she walks. He muses that "if a light shone from a house up a ways and the cry of a colicky baby caught her attention, she might step over to the house and call out softly to the woman inside trying to soothe the baby. The two of them might take turns massaging the infant['s] stomach, rocking, or trying to get a little soda water down . . . The woman could decide to go back to her house then, refreshed and ready to sleep, or she might keep her direction and walk further down . . . [o]n out, beyond the limits of the town, because *nothing at the edge thought she was prey*" (9; my italics).

The Ruby man's construction of 8-rock womanhood links ideal masculinity and the virtuous domestic utility of the 8-rock women. No "slack or sloven" women inhabit Ruby, he surmises, because "[f]rom the beginning its people were free and protected" (8). The link between the domestic productivity of the women and their free and protected status makes sense only within the context of his patriarchal ethos. Women will conform to their natural social roles, the reasoning goes, if men are adequate to the task of protecting and supporting them. This logic dictates that the unnamed speaker links the convent women's domestic inefficiency and alleged evil to the absence of men. The repetition of the phrase "nothing . . . thought she was prey" calls attention to the irony implicit in the Ruby man's perspective. Morrison riffs on the image of women as prey to undercut his romanticized gendered narrative. The real enemy of Ruby is not—as one of the Morgan twins intuits in an internal monologue—the white men who occasionally ride into town exposing their genitalia to defenseless young girls. Rather, it's the black leaders of Ruby who prey upon the weak and defenseless to maintain control over the town. Ironically, even as the unnamed speaker reflects on the goodness of the 8-rock women, he is preying upon unarmed women.

Although Deacon Morgan is the only man who ultimately takes moral responsibility for his actions, the narrative suggests that all these men are cognizant, on some conscious level, of what they are doing. While searching an upstairs bedroom, one of the Ruby men notices that all the mirrors in the room, except one, have been covered over with chalk. He deliberately looks away from the uncovered mirror because "[h]e does not want to see himself stalking females or their liquid." To look in the "uncovered" mirror would be to confront the reality of his violent attack on innocent women. In order for him to carry out the massacre of the women, then, he has to suppress the reality of his situation. It is "with relief"—the narrator repeats twice—that the disturbed man backs out of the room and "lets his handgun point down" (9).

Morrison's choice of Lone DuPres to reveal the story of the storming of the Convent emphasizes the importance of discarded knowledge in the black community. As the adopted daughter of Fairy DuPres, rescued from squalor and death while the original nine families were en route to Oklahoma, Lone is doubly marginalized in Ruby. Once a respected midwife, her services are no longer needed in the town, in part because she was blamed for the poor health of Sweetie Fleetwood's children, but primarily because a white hospital in a nearby town has begun accepting black patients. The women of Ruby prefer the hospital, Lone surmises, because it gives them a momentary break from their domestic responsibilities and because of the personal attention they receive. One such woman, Lone reports, "loved how people kept asking her how she felt." The men, for revealingly patriarchal reasons, prefer the hospital to Lone's midwifery because they enjoy "being in a place where other men were in charge instead of some toothless woman gumming gum to keep her gums strong" (271).

At once an outsider and insider, Lone possesses "something more profound than Morgan['s] memory or Pat Best's history book." She knows "the 'trick' of life and its 'reason'" (272). Lone elucidates the "trick" the nine Ruby men use to justify their slaying of the convent while eavesdropping on them as they plan their raid. "[T]here was no pity here," Lone reports, "when the men spoke of the ruination that was upon them—how Ruby was changing in intolerable ways—they did not think to fix it by extending a hand in fellowship or love. They mapped defense instead and honed evidence for its need, till each piece fit an already polished groove" (275). Predicated on 8-rock female virtue, the Ruby patriarchy provides a subterfuge to mask the men's self-serving motivations. They convince themselves that by murdering the Convent women they are safeguarding the moral and social integrity of Ruby. The "already polished groove" can be read as the ideology of black patriarchy which, naturalized as the social standard, affords the Ruby men a portable social script that, like the white male discourse on protecting white female virtue, can be appropriated to justify murder on moral grounds.

Eavesdropping on the nine men gathered at the Oven as they enumerate their reasons for wanting to dispose of the convent women, Lone intuits their intentions/motivations. She knows that Menus wishes to earn the respect of his father, who convinces him not to marry a "redbone" girl whom he loves. She is also aware of the shame that Menus harbors for having needed the convent women to help him recover from alcoholism. Not possessing "courage to leave and go on and live with the [redbone girl] someplace else," Menus submits to the "father's rule." Getting rid of some women "who had wiped up after him, washed his drawers, removed his vomit, listened to his curses as well as his sobs," explains Lone, "might convince him for a while that he was truly a man unpolluted by his mother's weakness, worthy of his father's patience [,] and that he was right to let the redbone go" (278).

Each of the men has his own reason for wanting the women killed. Harper wants somebody to blame for the failure of his first marriage; Wisdom Poole is looking for "a reason to explain why he had no control anymore over his brothers and sisters" (277); Sargeant wants to force Connie to sell him the convent land cheaply so that he will not have to pay for the use of her field to farm; K. D. seeks revenge for the humiliation he suffered at the hands of Gigi, a dweller at the Convent who rejects him; Jeff and Arnold Fleetwood "have been wanting to blame somebody for Sweetie's [sickly] children for a long time" (277). Finally, Deacon and Steward want to keep secret the sexual affair Deacon had with Connie, lest they fall victim to the political fate of their grandfather, Zechariah Morgan. "Neither one [of the Morgan twins]," reflects Lone, "put up with what he couldn't control" (279).

The second account of the raid (in Lone's chapter) revises the moral male-hero narrative by illuminating the sexual politics informing the Ruby men's violence. The second version *includes* the convent women's valiant defense/retaliation against their attackers, a crucial fact suppressed in the Ruby men's delineation of the event. The narrator reveals that as the men prepare to storm the convent they shoot open a "door that has never been locked" (285). Unlike the Ruby citizens, the convent women have never excluded anyone from living in their home. Read symbolically, the "door that has never been locked" represents a lost opportunity for reconciliation or at least understanding of the plight of the women. As Lone notes, the men never even consider this as a viable alternative to murder. That the men choose violence over peaceful resolution reveals their deep investment in maintaining their patriarchal authority and dominance.

Whereas the first version presents the women as passive victims, the counternarrative insists on realities suppressed by the patriarchal account. After the men enter the convent they are intercepted by the women. The narrator abandons the figurative language used to describe the men's killing of the white girl for a more literal prose, amplifying the material reality. The men's imagined liberation is set starkly against the women's material struggle for survival. Arnold Fleetwood is smashed over the head with "an alabaster ashtray" and the narrator notes that the woman "wielding it" was exhilarated by her act of violent retaliation. When Jeff Fleetwood attempts to shoot the woman who has brought his father to his knees, his aim is altered by another woman who hits his wrist with a pool cue stick. Before he can recover from the blow, another woman slams him over the head with a large picture frame. When Menus and Harper try to assist their fallen comrades, Harper is hit in the head with a skillet, which nearly knocks him unconscious. While trying to aid his wounded father, Menus is scalded when one of the women throws a pot of hot soup in his face. He is then stabbed with a butcher knife. The narrator reports that the knife goes so deep into Menus's shoulder that the woman wielding it "can't remove it for a second strike" (286). The graphic details deromanticize the black patriarchal discourse that frames the massacre of the Convent women as a revolutionary act of black liberation. In addition, it collapses the victimizer/victimized discourse which constructs women as ultimately powerless to combat the forces of patriarchy.

To fully understand the complicated relationship between black patriarchy and white supremacy in *Paradise,* however, it becomes important to understand Zechariah's function in the text. Heralded by Deek and Steward as the paragon of black manhood, Zechariah had been a successful politician in Louisiana until a political scandal—the details of which are never disclosed—leads to his ostracism by both blacks and whites. According to Deek Morgan, his grandfather became an "embarrassment to Negroes and both a threat and joke to whites. No one, black or white, could or would help him find other work. He was even passed up for a teaching job at a poor country primary school. The Negroes . . . took Zechariah's dignified manner for coldness and his studied speech for arrogance, mockery or both" (302). Unable to find work, he loses his nice house and is forced to move in with his sister. Nearly twenty years after being dismissed from office, Zechariah—then known as Coffee—is walking with his twin brother, Tea, when they are accosted by a group of young white boys who give them an ultimatum to either dance or get shot in the foot. Tea capitulates to the white men and dances, while Coffee opts to take the bullet in his foot. Unable to retaliate against the white boys, Coffee displaces his anger and shame onto his equally humiliated brother. As a result, Coffee changes his name to Zechariah and truncates his relationship with his brother, forbidding his children to mention their uncle's name.

When Zechariah's migrating group of "nine families and some more" reach the all-black town of Fairly, Oklahoma, they are turned away by lighter-skinned blacks who, having internalized white supremacy, reject them because of their dark skin. Ensconced in Haven and Ruby lore as the "Disallowing," this event becomes the unifying principle for the fifteen families in the group. The narrator observes that, after the Disallowing, "[t]hey became a tight band of wayfarers bound by the enormity of what had happened to them. *Their horror of whites was convulsive but abstract.* They saved the clarity of their hatred for the men who had insulted them in ways too confounding for language: first by excluding them, then by offering them staples to exist in that very exclusion" (189; my italics). Powerless to confront the real source of their angst in white men, the Haven men displace their feelings onto other black men who, like themselves, are victims of the same white supremacist culture. This explains why the "Disallowing" becomes celebrated as Haven-Ruby gospel, while the event between Zechariah and his brother is erased.

The Ruby men's feelings toward white men are further complicated by their internalization of a white patriarchal ethos. This psychosocial dynamic is most evident in the contradictory feelings Deek and Steward hold toward Reverend Misner. They are suspicious of Misner because they interpret his willingness to negotiate with white men—even though it is in pursuit of civil rights—as a weakness in his political thinking and moral character. Their biggest qualm about Misner, however, is that he opens a nonprofit credit union for his church members. They fear he might make the Rubians "think there was a choice about interest rates" (56).

Even as the twins openly express contempt for whites, they nevertheless repeat many of the same exploitive white financial practices in their dealings with other blacks. Revealingly, neither recognizes that his humanistic values have been compromised by economic greed. Steward—who has callously foreclosed on several Ruby properties—reflects nostalgically on the importance the Old Fathers placed on the sharing of community wealth. Driving home one night, he remembers that Haven "families shared everything [and] made sure no one was short. Cotton crop ruined? The sorghum growers split their profit with the cotton growers. A barn burned? The pine sappers made sure lumber 'accidentally' rolled off wagons at certain places to be picked up later that night . . . Having been refused by the world in 1890 on their journey to Oklahoma, Haven residents refused each other nothing, were vigilant to any need or shortage" (108–9).

In another telling example of how the Morgan twins repeat the exploitive financial practices of their white male counterparts, Deek chooses to open his bank on time rather than to assist Sweetie, whom he drives past as she walks aimlessly away from town. Even though Deek wonders why she is walking "coatless on a chilly October morning" far away from home after not having left her house in several years, he thinks, "[T]here should be *no* occasion when the bank of a good and serious town did not open on time" (114; my italics). Neither twin identifies the contradictions in their reading of the past or in their moral reasoning. It's no wonder that Misner, whose day-to-day affairs are consistent with his black nationalist politics, represents such a threat to them.

The extent of Steward's internalization of white male gender norms is revealed when he returns home after the meeting about the inscription on the Oven. Disgusted by the "cut-me-some-slack" attitude of the younger generation, Steward reflects on a curious act of bravery on the part of his oldest brother, Elder Morgan. A World War I veteran, Elder was walking the streets of New York City when he heard a commotion between two men and a prostitute. Unable to see the woman's face, he identified her as a prostitute from her attire and initially felt a "connection with the shouting [white] men." However, when he recognized that she was black, he became incensed. When the assailants knocked her to the pavement and attempted to kick her in the stomach, Elder interceded and punched one of them in the jaw. While Steward admires his brother's bravery, he does not readily identify with the powerlessness of the black woman. Rather, he feels an enmity so pronounced that he fantasizes about participating *with* the white men in the brutal assault. To Steward's thinking, the black prostitute represents all the negative characteristics whites associate with black people, particularly black women. He does not realize that this racialized reasoning—that the immoral acts of any black individual reflect poorly on the whole race—expresses an internalized white supremacy. His hatred of the black prostitute is linked to his desire to transcend the primitivistic stereotypes held by white America, a project that is strategically bankrupt because black individuality cannot be imagined within white supremacist ideology.

While her perspective is not utopian, Morrison does provide a vision of how the black community might begin a process of deprogramming that would allow it to imagine an alternative to patriarchy. The transformations of both Misner and Connie provide touchstones for reconceptualizing black manhood (and womanhood). These characters come to a level of spiritual and cultural self-awareness which allows them to confront the psycho-logical, spiritual, and emotional crises that affect them and their communities. Morrison links the problems of black patriarchy to emotional and psychological traumas of slavery that have gone unaddressed by both black men and women. She suggests that the reason black patriarchy remains largely unchallenged in the black community is that the coping mechanisms used to negotiate its postbellum traumas were fundamentally insufficient.

A key moment occurs when Misner observes that, for the Ruby men, "Booker T. *solutions* trumped Du Bois *problems* every time" (212; my italics). Morrison invokes the Washington–Du Bois de-bate to call attention to how the Ruby men suppress their trauma. Fundamentally, Washington's "solution" to black disenfranchise-ment by white America was for blacks to accept personal respon-sibility for remedying the socioeconomic problems they experi-enced after Reconstruction. Washingtonian racial uplift required blacks to "improve" themselves through rigorous moral training, emphasis on personal hygiene, and industrial education. For Mor-rison the problem with Washington's accommodationist politics is that they render invisible the mental and emotional stress expe-rienced by ex-slaves and ignore the "Catch-22" dynamic of white supremacy that defers the possibility of social equality for blacks. Conversely, Du Bois elucidates the complexity of this dynamic via his framing of "double consciousness." Blacks cannot attain "true self-consciousness," Du Bois argues, because they are forced to see themselves through "the revelation of the other [white] world," a world that constructs its implicit claim to racial superiority by invoking a fixed notion of black inferiority.

The psychosocial ramifications of employing Washington's ac-commodationist politics to address Du Boisian problems of sup-pressed psychological trauma are clearly illustrated by the Ruby men's response to the "Disallowing" and the convent women. Having failed to address adequately the suffering of their fathers during slavery or their own suffering during its violent aftermath, the Ruby men never comprehend their paradoxical love/hate relationship with whites. Their Washingtonian perspective provides them with a set of standards by which they can measure their progress as a race. Because of its emphasis on self-control and moral discipline, the Washingtonian approach furnishes the men with a temporary coping mechanism for their internalized feelings. Most critically, it allows them the illusion of self-determination. The omniscient narrator notes that the Old Fathers felt that "freedom was not entertainment, like a carnival or a hoedown that you can count on once a year. Nor was it the table droppings from the entitled. Here freedom was a test administered by the natural world that a man had to take for himself every day. And if he passed enough tests long enough, he was king" (99).

Having not experienced freedom as a "natural" phenomenon, the men embrace the Washingtonian notion that freedom/humanity is something to be earned. This thinking, which links the ability to acquire freedom with ideal manhood, obscures the dynamic of white supremacy, which reduces manhood, freedom, and humanity to the status of social commodities. In Freudian terms, the repressed and painful memories of slavery "return" in the acts of cruelty the black men unleash onto the women and each other. Thus links can be made between Zechariah Morgan's erasure of his twin brother from familial history and Haven-Ruby lore, Steward's empathy with the white men who brutally assault the black prostitute, the integration of the Disallowing into Ruby gospel, and the nine Ruby men's justification of the Convent massacre. Without a viable cultural means of addressing the psychological trauma, the men respond by repeating, rather than correcting, the abject cruelty of their white oppressors.

Morrison elucidates the complexity of the interracial love/hate relationship in her rendering of Connie's problematic relationship with her white mentor, Mary Magna. The scene in which Mary Magna rescues Connie from the streets of a coastal Brazilian city is described with stark irony. Even though "[b]y anyone's standard the snatching [of Connie and the other girls] was a rescue, because whatever life the exasperated, headstrong nun was dragging them to . . . would be superior to what lay before them in the shit-strewn paths of that city" (223), America produces another kind of poverty for these girls—namely, a cultural one. Invoking the Du Boisian model of double consciousness, Morrison describes the nuns' white supremacist theology. They seek "to bring God and language to natives who were assumed to have neither; to alter their diets, their clothes, their minds; to help them despise everything that had once made their lives worthwhile and to offer them instead the privilege of knowing the one and only God and a chance, thereby, for redemption" (227). Fundamentally, the nuns' theology links nonwhite cultures with savagery, primitivism, and sin. Cultural erasure becomes a prerequisite for "knowing" God. Moreover, "knowing" God entails acceptance of white supremacy. Despite the girls' improved economic status, they are being conditioned to "despise everything that had once made their lives worthwhile." Ultimately, Morrison asserts that cultural identity is crucial to the spiritual, emotional, and psychological well-being of blacks and nonwhites in America.

Connie's deep affection and respect for Mary Magna hamper her ability to recognize the extent of her ideological and cultural brainwashing. Even as Connie refers to her tutelage under Mary Magna as "[b]etter than all right," she "hardly noticed the things she was losing. The first to go were the rudiments of her first language. Every now and then she found herself speaking and thinking in that in-between place, the valley between the regulations of the first language and the vocabulary of the second" (242). Like the Ruby men, Connie is forced to negotiate the complexities of her life vis-à-vis a cultural and ideological vocabulary that constructs her original cultural heritage and language as primitive and savage. Therefore, when Connie discovers her power to resurrect the dead—a power that is linked to her African-Brazilian heritage— she believes that the power is evil despite Lone's insistence that "God don't make mistakes" (246). After Connie resurrects Deek and Soane Morgan's son, Scout, who "dies" in a car accident, she is momentarily exhilarated until she begins to consider the theological implications of her act. The narrator reports that "the exhilaration was gone now, and the thing seemed nasty to her. Like devilment. Like evil craft. Something it would mortify her to tell Mary Magna, Jesus, or the Virgin" (246). Even after Connie accepts Lone's spiritual tutelage and begins to practice her magic openly, she harbors fears that God will punish her for using her powers.

If Mary Magna embodies white supremacy, then Connie's obsessive efforts to keep her alive can be read—like the Ruby men's obsession with white supremacist patriarchy—as a desire to maintain the way of life that she has been conditioned to venerate. Her first attempt at healing Mary Magna is motivated by her "weakness of devotion turned to panic." Connie's subsequent efforts to keep her mentor alive are so intense that "Mary Magna [literally] glowed like a lamp till her very last breath" (247). Dependent on Mary Magna for spiritual and social guidance, Connie fails to negotiate her social and cultural reality on her own. Even as she accepts the "sympathy of her two friends, the help and murmurs of support from Mavis, [and] the efforts to cheer her from Grace," she feels that her "rope to the world had slid from her fingers." Without her mentor, Connie believes that she has "no identification, no insurance, no family, [and] no work" (247). Like her unhealthy obsession with Deek, Connie's attachment to Mary Magna reveals the extent of her investment in white supremacist and patriarchal ideologies. Instead of focusing her anger on her mentor or ex-lover, Connie begins to resent the other women in the convent. Binging on alcohol, she wishes that "she had the strength to beat the life out of the women freeloading in the house" (248). Like the Ruby men, she displaces her angst onto weaker individuals.

Morrison allows Connie access to her lost cultural heritage via an erotic encounter with a spiritual presence that, with eyes "as round and green as new apples," resembles a male version of herself. By personifying Connie's repressed cultural "ego" as male, and portraying her encounter with that "ego" as sexual, Morrison rewrites Connie's problematic relationship with Deek. While not fully developed, Connie's relationship with her spiritual ego suggests that one must love one's self and culture in order to attain spiritual wholeness.

Similarly, Morrison's rendering of Connie's relationship with her spiritual ego also revises Mary Magna's association of savagery and primitivism with the material and cultural African body. Once Connie completes her transformation into Consolata Sosa, she warns the convent women, "Never break them in two. Eve is Mary's mother. Mary is the daughter of Eve" (263). As Kubitschek observes in her analysis of *Paradise,* Consolata "specifically denies the body/soul opposition central to Mary Magna's Catholicism. Recognizing the Virgin Mary and Eve as symbols of womanhood, divided into good and evil, Consolata rejoins them" (182). Consolata successfully negotiates the white supremacist ideology of her mentor and emerges as the "new and revised Reverend Mother" (265).

While less fully developed, Morrison's rendering of Misner's transformation also points beyond the white supremacist and patriarchal impasse. Unlike Connie, Misner is partially cognizant of the ways in which blacks have internalized white supremacy. Prior to his spiritual epiphany he believes that "whites not only had no patent on Christianity. . . [but] were often its obstacle." Jesus, Misner thinks, "had been freed from white religion" (209). Despite his political awareness, Misner is blind to the patriarchal thinking that undergirds his black nationalistic perspective. This becomes evident during his eulogy for Save-Maria, Jeff and Sweetie Fleetwood's youngest child who dies of an unexplained illness. While preaching, Misner reflects on the pomposity of the eight Ruby leaders in attendance. He notes that the men "think they have outfoxed the whiteman when in fact they imitate him. They think they are protecting their wives and children, when in fact they are maiming them. And when the maimed children ask for help, they look elsewhere for the cause" (306). Unaware of his own patriarchal thinking, Misner preaches a sermon that reinforces their beliefs. Rather than celebrate Save-Maria's short life, he laments her death as if it were a wasted resource.

At the end of his sermon, however, Misner has a spiritual vision much like the one he experienced with Anna when they made the trip to the Convent after the massacre. The vision allows him to identify his complicity, compelling him to preach a second sermon that fundamentally negates his first. "It is our own misfortune," Misner admonishes, "if we do not know in our long life what she [Save-Maria] knew every day of her short one: that although life in life is terminal and life after life is everlasting, He is with us always, in life, after it and especially in between, lying in wait for us to know the splendor" (307). Reworking the central themes of Consolata's sermon to the convent women, Morrison uses Misner's sermon to revise the Ruby men's Washingtonian view of God, manhood, and freedom as commodities to be earned. Misner realizes that such thinking minimizes the importance of Save-Maria's short life. Moreover, it forestalls the process of spiritual healing for the Ruby men because it constructs God as a kind of brash dictator who gauges the importance of his underlings in accordance with their moral and social merit. Unchallenged white supremacist notions of patriarchy, God, and freedom have produced a sense of entitlement in the Ruby men that resembles that of their white oppressors.

Morrison implies that the Ruby men, like the Convent women, must come to terms with their cultural and historical roots if they are to effectively negotiate the lingering effects of their slave legacy. She delineates her political message via Deek's break with his brother Steward. Hoping to identify the spiritual presence that Connie was addressing before she was shot by his brother, Deek seeks out Misner for spiritual counseling. To signal the dawn of what might grow into a new era in Ruby, Morrison has Deek replay his grandfather's legendary two-hundred-mile barefoot trek to Oklahoma in his own barefoot trek through the heart of town to Misner's house. This revision of Zechariah's barefoot walk calls attention to the social bankruptcy of the legend. Deek's therapeutic session with Misner forecasts the possibility of patriarchal reform in Ruby. Crucially, Deek realizes that the New Fathers of

Ruby have become like their white oppressors: "the kind of [men] who set [themselves] up to judge, rout and even destroy the needy, the defenseless, the different" (302). But, even as Deek recognizes the moral destructiveness of his patriarchal thinking, he has difficulty coming to terms with his ancestral past. He is particularly perplexed by his grandfather's decision to erase his brother from Morgan history. Although Deek doesn't resolve his issues with his grandfather, Morrison suggests that Misner's guidance will assist him in coming to a productive and healthy understanding. When Deek admits to Misner that he has "got a long way to go" in regard to revising his masculine ethos, Misner replies optimistically, "You'll make it . . . No doubt about it" (303).

Clearly, Morrison's critique of black patriarchy provides crucial insights into the problematic ways that black men conceptualize manhood. Most significantly, she outlines the various cultural and social obstacles that impede the construction of a viable notion of black manhood, showing the extent to which black men's gender identity is inextricably bound up with those of their white male counterparts. Her remedy to the problem of black male identity, however, is certainly more vision than blueprint, as she offers African cultural reclamation as the solution to renegotiating black gender identities. Premised on the idea of a monolithic and uncomplicated African cultural identity, this solution is irreparably flawed. Not only does it fail to account for the complexity and variety of African cultures, it ignores the difficulty that blacks, who are several generations removed from their cultural origins, would incur trying to access their lost cultural heritage.

Despite its theoretical complications, *Paradise* furnishes a useful and productive framework from which to engage the psychosocial implications of patriarchy for black men. Most importantly, Morrison underscores the ways in which internalized white supremacy and concomitant cultural erasure complicate the process of dismantling black patriarchy. Her portrayal of the town's response to the raid on the Convent bears this out. The vast majority of Ruby men *and* women continue to endorse the black patriarchal ethos, as demonstrated by how "rapidly" the fabricated accounts of the raid on the Convent were "becoming gospel" in the town. The narrator reports that "every one of the assaulting men had a different tale and their families and friends (who had been nowhere near the Convent) supported them, enhancing, recasting, inventing misinformation" (297). The most important lesson Morrison offers in *Paradise* is that one cannot effectively address patriarchal thinking in the black community without first engaging the social, economic, psychological, cultural, and gender dynamics that maintain its existence. To do so is to ignore critical variables that allow patriarchy to sustain itself.

4

"SO MUCH OF WHAT WE KNOW AIN'T SO"
The Other Gender in Toni Cade Bambara's *The Salt Eaters*

> [W]hen they [whites] got you thinking that they're to blame for *every*thing
> they have you thinking they's some kind of gods! . . . Then you begins to
> think up evil and begins to destroy everybody around you, and you blames
> it on crackers. *Shit!* Nobody as powerful as we make them out to be. We
> got our own *souls*, don't we?
>
> ALICE WALKER, *The Third Life of Grange Copeland*

IN *THE SALT EATERS* (1980), her first and most highly regarded
novel, Toni Cade Bambara provides critical insights into the cultural variables that frustrate gender relations in the black community. In particular, she dramatizes how black men and women
impose unrealistic gender standards on each other that foster intraracial conflicts and violence. Unable and, at times, unwilling to
address these intraracial gender conflicts, her characters become
co-conspirators in their own racial and/or gender oppression.
Though Bambara certainly emphasizes the problematics of black
male victimhood and privilege, her aim is not to place the onus
on black men. Rather she wants to illuminate how internalized
"white supremacist" notions of gender roles have fostered—and
foster—intraracial gender and cultural unrest. To this end, she
does not simply replace the victimized black male motif (which
absolves black men of moral and social responsibility because of
racial oppression) with a version emphasizing black female victimhood. She strives instead to establish modes of cultural analysis
that will empower blacks across gender differences. Her critique
reveals that black feminist discussions that address black men as
if they enjoyed the racial privileges of white men are as problematic as the black nationalist discourse that labels any woman who

takes initiative an emasculator. It becomes clear that neither black men nor black women will achieve real understanding on gender issues if they ignore the racial and gender ideologies that inform their perceptions of each other.

In *The Salt Eaters* Bambara attempts to reconcile these issues by introducing a vision of black cultural restoration premised on the existence of a real and accessible ancestral power latent within black Americans. Remarking on the cultural vision in the novel, Bambara explains, "What compelled me to tackle [the issue of cultural wholeness] . . . in *Salt* was the amount of psychic and spiritual damage that is being done to us, and the fact that we're encouraged to ignore or laugh at the damage" (Chandler, 348). Bambara argues that achieving this cultural wholeness comes at a high social cost. In effect, those who acquire it must accept responsibility for self-determination and cultural determination, rejecting as they do the idea that oppression (of any sort) robs them of social agency. For these reasons, Bambara observes, most blacks do not desire wholeness. She writes, "To be *whole*—politically, psychically, spiritually, culturally, intellectually, aesthetically, physically, and economically whole—is of profound significance. It is significant because there is a correlative to this. There is a responsibility to self and to history that is developed once you are 'whole,' once you are well, once you acknowledge your powers" (348). Acknowledging the existence and viability of these cultural powers is for Bambara the first and most significant move toward achieving cultural healing and wholeness.

Most critics who engage the gender-cultural politics in *The Salt Eaters* focus on Bambara's treatment of black women's subjugation within and beyond the black community. This trend is best illustrated in Ann Folwell Stanford's essay "He Speaks for Whom? Inscription and Reinscription of Women in *Invisible Man* and *The Salt Eaters*" and Elliott Butler-Evans's critical study *Race, Gender and Desire*. Attentive to the problematic representations of black women in texts by black male authors, Stanford discusses *The Salt Eaters* as a gendered corrective text to Ralph Ellison's *Invisible*

Man. She argues that Bambara revises Ellison's stereotypical representations of black women like Mary Rambo (a mammy figure) with more complex and fully actualized black female characters like the spiritual healer Minnie Ransom. To this end, Stanford suggests, Bambara "demonstrates a strategy used by many other women writers to critique and correct textual records that perpetuate destructive and essentialized sexual stereotypes" (29).

Like Stanford, Butler-Evans also emphasizes Bambara's redeeming representation of black women. Highlighting Bambara's treatment of sexism in the black community, he contends that the chief political aim in *The Salt Eaters* is to illuminate the problem of black women's empowerment, especially as it concerns the cultural expectations of black female self-sacrifice. He insists that Velma's mental breakdown and attempted suicide should be read as a "serious questioning of the wisdom of self-negation in the interest of a totalizing [black nationalist] ideology and a rebellion against it" (181). Ultimately, he concludes that Velma should be understood as a hero rather than as a culturally misguided activist.

Even as they have provided valuable insights and evoked animated discussions regarding Bambara's feminist politics, critics have for the most part not generated in-depth analysis of the male characters' gender-racial crises. This is a significant oversight, given that Bambara sees the plight of black women as inextricably and intimately linked with that of black men. To gain a more complete understanding and appreciation for the complexity of Bambara's feminist politics, it becomes necessary to examine her intersecting model of black gender roles. Such an examination is critical because it not only shows how black women who are conscious of intraracial gender hierarchies get ensnared into policing rather than challenging their prescribed gender roles. It exposes the ways that even black men who are sensitive to the suffering of black women replay and reify debilitating notions of black womanhood.

In *The Black Woman* (1970), Bambara's groundbreaking anthology on black women's issues, she asserts that it "doesn't take any particular expertise to observe that one of the most characteristic features of our community is the antagonism between our men and our women" (107). These gender tensions are exacerbated by the mixed gender messages that are passed down from generation to generation: "Mamma tells junior his father was a no-good bum and then proceeds to groom him to be just like his daddy, an abuser of young girls, but faithful of course to Mamma. Mamma tells daughter that men ain't no damn good and raises such suspicions and fears and paranoia in her heart that she is nasty as hell to men she meets and elicits lousy behavior" (106). This destructive pattern produces male-female relationships in which intimacy is built upon a volatile finance-romance struggle, or as Bambara puts it plainly: "her [the black woman] trying to get into his [the black man's] pocket, [and] him trying to get into her drawers" (106). Operating from a romanticized notion of Africa, she contends that these tensions between black men and women result from centuries of white supremacist programming. Black folks have "been programmed to depend on white models [of manhood and womanhood] or white interpretations of non-white models" to establish their own identities. When white Westerners colonized Africa, Bambara argues, they disrupted the matriarchal African system by introducing the concept of property. "Property led to class divisions which disrupted the communal society. To guarantee the transmission of property, patrilineal inheritance was adopted. To ensure a clear line of inheritance, the woman's liberty and mobility, especially sexual, was curtailed through monogamy. The nuclear family cut her off from the larger society and turned this homebody into a nobody" (104). Men were conditioned to believe that their natural obligation was to support their families financially, while women were taught that their obligation was to serve the family. "Just as the 'natives' became the white man's burden, his property, she [the woman] became the man's burden, his Mrs., and the children became the parents' burden" (104).

Bambara contends that to rectify this problem of Western conditioning blacks need to reject white gender roles and focus instead on a commitment to the struggle of black liberation. She cites several prominent black activists of the 1960s, including Malcolm X, Muhammad Ali, Abbey Lincoln, Kathleen Cleaver, and Nina Simone, as examples of individuals who have begun this process of gender-cultural deprogramming. These black activists, she insists, have supplanted the sexually exploitive markers of manhood and the tragic, "whitified" markers of womanhood with new models of gender roles that were measured by one's "commitment to the Struggle." She maintains, however, that during the late sixties most black men bought into ideologies that portrayed black women as "evil matriarchs" and parasitical welfare mothers. As a result of these messages, black men indulged "in lost-balls fantasies and attempt[ed] to exact recompense by jumping feet foremost into her [woman's] chest, and she start[ed] conjuring up abandonment stories and ADC nightmares and leap[t] at his throat." Both men and women began to act as if they were "personae in some historical melodrama" (109).

To resolve these gendered cultural dilemmas, Bambara argues, black men and women need "to keep the big guns on the real enemy"—white male supremacy. Most important, "men have got to develop some heart and some sound analysis to realize that when sisters get passionate about themselves and their direction, it does not mean they're readying up to kick men's ass. They're readying up for honesty. And women have got to develop some heart and some sound analysis so they can resist the temptation of buying peace with their man with self-sacrifice and posturing. The job then regarding 'roles' is to submerge breezy definitions of manhood/womanhood . . . until realist definitions emerge through a commitment to Blackhood" (109). Fundamentally, Bambara believes that this gender-racial liberation must be ushered in with individual self-analysis, not finger pointing or scapegoating on either side of the gender line. Delineating a model for liberation reliant upon individual empowerment, she contends that "[r]evolution begins with the self, in the self. The individual, the basic revolutionary unity, must be purged of poison and lies that assault the ego and threaten the heart, that hazard the next larger unit—the couple or pair, that jeopardize the still larger unit—the family or cell, that put the movement at peril" (109).

Bambara's treatment of her male characters' identity crises in *The Salt Eaters* allows a fuller understanding of her racial-gender politics. Using Bambara's detailed (and too often ignored) analysis of black male–female antagonisms in the *Black Woman* as a guidepost, this chapter addresses the historical and cultural phenomena that complicate any attempt at overhauling these destructive gender roles. Close scrutiny of Velma's relationship with her sister Palma and her godmother Sophie reveals the ways in which Velma unintentionally reifies self-deprecating notions of black womanhood. Foregrounding this aspect of Velma's ideology brings James/Obie's (hereafter just James) and Fred Holt's gender-race crises into focus. Both men, in strikingly different ways, perceive themselves as victims of a monolithic white supremacist regime. Though they are justified in their perceptions, their parochial and, at times, essentialized views of white supremacy and black male victimhood forestall their processes of cultural growth. These distorted views of white supremacy and black male victimhood allow James to erase the suffering of a black woman who is raped by his brother Roland. Moreover, these views help him to substantiate his belief that black women have conspired against him to prevent him from fathering a child. Unlike James, who blames black women for his feelings of emasculation, Fred scapegoats his white wife. Oblivious to the racial politics that inform his choice to marry a white woman, Fred has difficulty comprehending the cultural advice of his best friend Porter, who rightly identifies Fred's racial inferiority complex. Like Velma, James and Fred are blind to the ways that they are deeply complicit in their own racial-gender oppression.

The two stories of women-in-crisis that Minnie Ransom—the spiritual healer of the community—relays to Velma during the earliest stages of her healing process contextualize Velma's identity crisis. The first involves a woman who seeks a quick fix to the emotional pain of losing her mother. In the second, a woman goes after her husband with a hammer after misinterpreting the meaning of a folk song. Outlining the obstacles that impede cultural healing, the first narrative identifies how "whitified" notions of self and reality have stunted the emotional and psychological growth and development of the black community. The second shows how this stunted growth and development contribute to the perpetuation of intraracial gender antagonisms. Taken together, the narratives illuminate the source and complexity of Velma's mental breakdown and attempted suicide.

Bambara highlights the obstacles that hamper cultural healing in Minnie's conversation with the woman in mourning. When the woman asks Minnie if she has a pill that can ease her pain following her recent loss of her mother, the spiritual healer diagnoses and diagrams the sentiment underlying her request: "Wanted a pill cause she was in pain, felt bad, wanted to feel good" (8). Relaying the story directly to Velma, Minnie narrates her response to the woman: "So I say, 'Sweetheart, what's the matter?' And she says 'My mama died and I feel so bad, I can't go on' and dah dah dah. Her mama died, she's *supposed* to feel bad. Expect to feel good when ya mama's gone! Climbed right into my lap . . . Two hundred pounds of grief and heft if she was one-fifty. Bless her heart, just a babe of the times. Wants to be smiling and feeling good all the time. Smooth sailing as they lower the mama into the ground" (8–9).

Here, Minnie observes that mourning the death of loved ones is as natural and necessary a part of life as death itself. The grieving woman's desire to bypass this necessary process represents for Minnie a failure on the younger generation's part to connect with the teachers, loas, messengers, and cultural healers of the community. Underscoring Minnie's perspective on this generational failure, the narrator reports that the bearers of culture were so seldom and inappropriately used that they "were beginning to believe [that] their calling in life was to keep a lover from straying, make a neighbor's hair fall out in fistfuls, swat horses into a run just so and guarantee the number for the day" (146).

Bambara and Minnie imply that the inability of blacks to usefully access or utilize their ancestral powers is inextricably linked to their acceptance of white-centered cultural values and consciousness. That is, blacks do not seek cultural-specific answers to their social and political queries because they have been conditioned to venerate the dominant culture's notions of self and reality and treat their African history and ancestry with suspicion and shame. Viewing themselves through the lens of their oppressors, blacks accept their subordinate status as inevitable and, to some extent, warranted. Thereby they resign themselves to a life of mediocrity.

With this ideological outlook, avoiding rather than addressing suffering becomes the primary pursuit of many. Minnie implies that the woman in mourning acts like a child because her inability to fully comprehend her cultural legacy and power has stunted her emotional and psychological growth. Though this woman does seek out a cultural healer for assistance, her ultimate goal is not to understand the significance of her mother's death but simply to put an end to her personal suffering. She acknowledges the existence of such cultural resources, but doesn't understand how they can help her to gain a healthier, more enlightened vision of herself and the world around her.

In Minnie's second narrative Bambara highlights how this stunted emotional and psychological growth fosters intraracial gender dilemmas. The woman who attacks her husband with a hammer interprets the words to a folk song—"There's a hole in the bucket, dear Liza, dear Liza, Well, fix it, dear Henry"—to mean that her husband is responsible for fulfilling her material, sexual, and emotional needs. Thus, when he fails to live up to what she thinks are his "natural" responsibilities, she tries to hammer him into compliance. Illuminating the shortsightedness of this woman's perspective, Minnie observes, "Full-grown women talking about a song told her to hit her husband in the head. Like she don't have options" (44). She then offers an Afrocentric and empowering reading of the song: "Just like Liza in the song. She can just go ahead and fix the fool bucket herself and quit getting so antsy about it. Or she can go find a man that can. Always got options"

(44). She continues, "Ole no-count Henry [the husband] ain't the only reality . . . she might try affirming his ability to wield a hammer or tote her some water and see what that'll do" (44). Finally, she concludes, "I don't understand these women sometime. Baby a man and then get all in a stiff cause he don't know how to fix a hole in the bucket. Sometime original mother is too much the mother, if you know what I mean" (45).

Advancing Bambara's cultural thesis, Minnie calls attention to the destructive consequences that result when black women (and men) can no longer properly "read" or comprehend their cultural heritage. The woman in this scenario has so deeply accepted the cultural limitations imposed upon her that she is unable to imagine the options she has regarding her relationship with her husband. Given her state of mind, it stands to reason that she would resort to violence in order to force her husband into compliance; she believes that she is exercising the only option that she has available. If she comprehended her cultural powers, Minnie (and Bambara) argue, she would recognize the extent of her social and personal agency. Recognizing this agency would allow her to see that she ultimately does not need a man to achieve sexual, material, or emotional satisfaction. Moreover, this recognition would alert her to how she and other black women enable the kind of social behavior that she abhors in black men. To acknowledge complicity in these gender dilemmas, then, is crucial to self-empowerment and cultural empowerment.

These two scenarios illuminate how intraracial gender antagonisms are created and maintained. In particular, they suggest that black men and women have not yet learned to distinguish between what I call "unnecessary" and "necessary" suffering. "Necessary" suffering suggests that the process of rejecting "whitified" models of womanhood and manhood, though empowering for both men and women, will ultimately require a level of suffering and sacrifice on both their parts. In contrast, "unnecessary" suffering suggests that blacks incur avoidable hardships and pain because they are blind to the ways that these "whitified" models of gender inform their (mis)treatment of each other.

In an interview with Claudia Tate, Bambara speaks to the dynamics of necessary suffering when she observes that "[a]nything of value is going to cost you something" (16). This relationship between value and cost is clearly evident in Bambara's treatment of cultural healing in *The Salt Eaters*. In counseling Velma and the woman in mourning, Minnie explains that suffering is an essential component of healing. She refers to these phenomena of suffering as the "burdens of the healthy": the notion that physical, mental, and emotional suffering are the requisite cost of cultural wholeness. Sophie makes a similar observation during a spiritual conversation with Velma when she says, "Not all wars have causalities . . . Some struggles between old and new ideas, some battles between ways of seeing have only victors. Not all dying is the physical self" (219). Ostensibly, Sophie reveals that not all cultural or gender conflicts are essentially negative; that certain kinds of suffering are even important and necessary to advancing ideas regarding the black struggle.

Unlike necessary suffering, however, unnecessary suffering has no redeeming cultural benefits. It results when blacks begin to view their social and cultural struggles as static and unchangeable. The narrator records this process: "So used to being unwhole and unwell one forgot what it was to walk upright and see clearly, breathe easily, think better than was taught, be better than one was programmed to believe . . . For people sometimes believed that it was safer to live with complaints, was necessary to cooperate with grief . . . [and] become . . . an accomplice in self-ambush" (107). This "self-ambush" is largely responsible for intraracial gender and cultural conflicts. Having unintentionally severed their connection with their cultural heritage and spirituality, blacks construct unrealistic and damaging images of themselves and their gender counterparts. Therefore they impose unrealistic and unhealthy gender standards on themselves and each other that ultimately sustain and perpetuate gender and cultural antagonisms. This type of suffering is unnecessary, as Minnie and Bambara argue, because blacks have the option to reject these notions of self and reality. Ultimately, blacks do not exercise their options because they have reconciled themselves to a life of perpetual hardships and disappointment.

Bambara suggests that undoing this process of self-ambush requires blacks to actively pursue alternatives to white-centered social, cultural, and gender realities. The necessity and importance of this active pursuit are implicit in Minnie's original question to Velma: "Are you sure, sweetheart, that you want to be well?" (3). If Velma answers "yes" to this question, then the implication is that she must consciously choose to do something about her "illness." Given that this illness stems in large part from her own self-ambush (as I will explain in greater detail below), she must actively pursue ways to reverse the process of unnecessary suffering in her life.

Like the two women-in-crisis, Velma (in her earlier stages of healing) is unable to distinguish between necessary and unnecessary suffering. Thus she strikes out at black men, whom she perceives as the root cause of her emotional and social pain. Her spirited indictment of the male leaders of the Claybourne activist group is very telling in this regard. Lambasting the male leaders of the group for abusing their male privilege, Velma rallies most of the female members to break with the organization. After announcing the plans for the split she remarks facetiously, "You all continue lollygagging at Del Giorgio's, renting limousines and pussyfooting around town profiling in your three-piece suits and imported pajamas while the people sweat it out through hard times" (37). The reader is never presented with a view of the Claybourne men that substantiates Velma's indictment of them. Rather, the male privilege that she highlights takes place during a political rally that she attends prior to this meeting. That she appears to confuse the accounts may explain why her sister Palma "yank[s] her down in her chair" before she finishes enumerating their alleged infractions against the women (37).

Critiquing Velma's and the sisters of the yam's response to the male Claybourne leaders, Keith Byerman asserts that Velma's indictment of black male privilege reinforces rather than challenges black patriarchy because she, like the other sisters of the yam, employ "ahistorical forms of power" that are culturally vacuous. The problem with their system of thought "lies not in the values of such systems [feminism, capitalism, ecology, etc.], but in their separation from the black roots of these ideas." While their complaints of exploitation are certainly valid, their method of responding to male domination reifies the very notions of power they seek to eliminate. For Byerman "their resistance consists of accepting the principle of domination and subordination and simply reversing the direction of oppression. In doing so, they perpetuate the very system that has so adversely affected them" (125).

Though Byerman is attentive to the ways that the women reinforce patriarchal power, he stops short of engaging the gender-specific complexities inherent in the women's response to the men and to each other. He ignores the gender suffering that generates the women's antagonisms against the men and amongst themselves. As a result, Byerman slips into a version of the gender trap that he astutely identifies. Without offering a critique of black male identity, he contends that it is James/Obie's role to "call forth the spirit of healing" in the black community "since his name [Obie] makes him the obeah man, the conjurer of African and African-American folk belief" (127). As will be demonstrated later, James's deeply problematic perception of black women as emasculators and "baby killers" makes him an unlikely candidate to usher in a new liberation movement.

In *Sister of the Yam* bell hooks situates the response of Velma and the sisters of the yam to black male privilege in a gender-specific and historical context. Outlining what she calls the "myth of the strong black woman," hooks observes that, since the early days of slavery, black women have had to share in the back-breaking jobs of their male counterparts and shoulder responsibility for the emotional and financial upkeep of the family. They have maintained this unhealthy pattern of servitude for so long that they "often do not know how to set protective boundaries that would eliminate certain forms of stress in . . . [their] lives" (55). Overhauling this myth is complicated, hooks explains, because society rewards black women when they are willing to push themselves beyond healthy limits. Moreover, many black women accept and perpetuate this myth because it helps them sustain the notion that their mental toughness allows them to overcome any obstacle—social, financial, or familial.

Velma's indictment of her sister Palma for not living up to this image demonstrates the tenacity of the myth hooks outlines. Reflecting on her sister's decision to stay at home and paint rather than participate in the political march, Velma condemns what she perceives as her sister's lack of political commitment. To commemorate her feeling of betrayal, Velma purchases Palma cowrie-shell bracelets at the march and then gives it to her under false pretenses as a gift. Underscoring the symbolic meaning and intent of the bracelet, Velma muses:

> MATRIARCHAL CURRENCY, the sign on the table had read. And she'd purchased the cowrie-shell bracelets for Palma less as a memento [and] more as a criticism. Bought the cowrie shells to *shame* her, for she should've been on the march, had no right to the cool solitude of her studio painting pictures of sailboats while sisters were being beat and raped, and workers shot and children terrorized. "Divination tools," she had winked at the peddler who'd been too eager to rap the long rap about cowries and matriarchy. Velma'd worn them that day in the park and for the duration of the march to the state capitol to set up tents. "Little pussies with stitched teeth," her aide on the PR committee had leered, touching the cowries. (36; my italics)

Despite Velma's attack, Palma is very politically active in and outside the Claybourne community. In fact, she takes Velma's place in the radical, all-female political troupe The Seven Sisters. Velma's resentment toward her sister, then, reveals more about the tenacity of the myth of the strong black woman than it does about Palma's level of political commitment. While Velma experiences her resentment toward Palma as gender-cultural betrayal, the source of her angst is really envy. Unlike Velma, Palma has learned to negotiate her obligation to self and community in a healthy and productive way. Unable to achieve the same level of negotiation, Velma attempts to police her sister into conformity by shaming her. The words Velma uses to describe her sister's respite are revealing. She states that Palma "had no right" to set aside time to engage in her hobby of painting, because she was needed on the frontlines of the liberation struggle. Clearly, Velma reproduces and reinforces the self-sacrificing image of black women as what Zora Neale Hurston's narrator in *Their Eyes Were Watching God* calls "mules of the world." In effect, she condemns Palma for taking time out from her political and social obligations for self-fulfilling experiences. In this way, Velma becomes an active agent in perpetuating the very myth that causes her suffering and forecloses the possibility of cultural healing.

Bambara indicates the social currency that Velma receives for her gendered suffering in her treatment of Sophie's relationship with Portland Edgers. A race man, Edgers is forced at gunpoint to assault Sophie, Velma's godmother, during a political protest. When Velma sees Edgers working in Sophie's yard after the incident, she becomes incensed. "'Got his nerve,' Velma had said [to Sophie], wiping her feet on the mat as if to kick up dust and jute in Edgers's face. 'How could he look you in the eye after what he's done?'" When Sophie asks Velma what he has done, she becomes even more enraged: "What's he done!" Velma retorts, "That bastard ought to cut off both his hands" (151). She then closes her eyes "as if the *mere thought* of Sophie's terror was too much to bear even in memory, even secondhand" (151). Significantly, Velma never actually identifies what unforgivable crime Edgers has committed, or even pursues an explanation from her godmother as to why she does not hold him to blame. Instead, she appears to revel in the "mere thought" of the terror Sophie experiences.

The starkly ironic language that Bambara uses to frame Velma's response shows that she benefits, socially and personally, from assuming the martyr role. That the narrator describes Velma's experience of Sophie's terror as "secondhand" is especially telling. The term calls attention to Velma's appropriation of her godmother's experience of suffering to reinforce her own overused and uncritical narrative about black male oppression. Most crucially, however, it exposes the dynamics that sustain the strong black woman myth. In effect, by choosing to adhere to the "rumor version" of the beating rather than to get a firsthand account of the events from Sophie, Velma enforces the victimized subtext of this myth premised on suffering.

Aware of what Velma is doing, Sophie becomes infuriated. Specifically, she recognizes that Velma is more concerned about her own personal suffering than that of the people most directly impacted by the event. These people include Sophie's son Smitty, who is paralyzed from the waist down because of a severe beating he takes at the hands of the white police. The narrator reports that during Velma's indictment of Edgers, Sophie wants to "grab her by the shoulders and shake her, shake her for Smitty, shake her for Edgers, herself, shake her till her head flopped. Edgers had had a pistol to his neck but had refused to go on beating her and been beaten himself" (151). Sophie compares Velma to the biblical character Lot's wife, who is turned into a pillar of salt because she disregards God's command not to look back at the burning city of Sodom and Gomorrah. She argues that Velma has been "ossified" by her past experiences: "Wasn't that what happened to Lot's Wife? A loyalty to old things, a fear of the new, a fear to change, to look ahead?" (152).

Sophie's assessment of Velma's behavior suggests that Velma did not pursue a firsthand account of the events because she was afraid that her godmother's account would not coincide with the rumored or secondhand version she *chooses* to accept. Having to contend with the reality of the situation would force her to reevaluate her views on black men and self-sacrifice. Because, as bell hooks demonstrates, martyrdom operates as the social pay-off for extensive self-sacrifice, Sophie's firsthand version would require Velma to relinquish her primary means of cultural reward and her justification for overcommitting herself. Lacking self-love, this realization for Velma would prove disastrous, emotionally and mentally, as it eventually does in her attempted suicide.

Velma's identity crisis aside, this episode between Sophie and Edgers embodies the cultural drama that Bambara outlines in her discussion of black male versus female antagonisms. That a white sheriff forces Edgers to beat Sophie by holding a gun to his head directly links black male abuse of black women to white male oppression. Bambara complicates this connection when Edgers turns against the sheriff at the risk of his own life—an act that ultimately results in his being pistol-whipped along with Sophie and thrown in jail.

Read intertexually, Edgers's response to the sheriff invokes the advice on "real manhood" that Grange Copeland, in Alice Walker's *The Third Life of Grange Copeland* (1970), gives his son Brownfield, who uses racism as an excuse for why he murders his own wife. Directing his comments to his granddaughter Ruth (Brownfield's daughter) while his son listens on, Grange declares, "The white folks could have forced him [Brownfield] to live in shacks; they might have even forced him to beat his wife and children like they was dogs, so he could keep on feeling something less than shit. But where was the *man* in him that let Brownfield *kill* his wife? What cracker pulled the trigger? And if a cracker did cause him to kill his wife, Brownfield should have turned the gun on himself, for he wasn't no man. He *let* the cracker hold the gun, because he was too weak to distinguish that cracker's will from his!" (289).

Brownfield becomes what bell hooks calls a "surrogate oppressor" when he displaces his feelings of emasculation on to his wife. As such, he becomes complicit in perpetuating white social dominance. By contrast, the *man* in Edgers refuses to capitulate to the ideologies of white dominance that would have him continue to attack Sophie. In effect, Edgers is able to distinguish "his will" from the "cracker's will" in that he turns against the sheriff at the risk of his own life. The kind of "manhood" that is exemplified in this instance brings into focus the idea of "necessary" suffering that undergirds Bambara's gender politics. Although turning against the sheriff brings the officer's wrath upon Edgers and Sophie, the act disrupts the ideological cycle that fosters social and political discord between black men and women. As a result, their shared, necessary suffering draws them closer together and helps them empathize with each other across gender differences.

Ultimately, Bambara demonstrates that blacks have the mental and cultural capacity to resist and reverse the effects of white social dominance in their lives. In the most poignant moment in the novel, Bambara stages the process of healing that takes place between Edgers and Sophie following their ordeal:

> Edgers was standing by the pole beans scraping his work boots against the edge of her brick walk, and she held her breath as his words floated towards her. "Get used to me please, Sophie" was all it was. Then turning to attend to things: mending the fence, liming the trees, sharpening her ax for her, turning over the earth, dumping out sacks of bonemeal, chicken droppings, a compost of his making that would promote new growth, new life. And no sense telling him he needn't, cause he needed, and she knew it each time she combed her hair, and she needed. "Get used to me please, Sophie," he had said after all this time. She thought she had. (151)

To make amends for his participation in Sophie's beating during the march, Edgers takes responsibility for the upkeep of her property. Though Sophie recognizes the extreme duress that caused Edgers to strike her, she honors his request to make amends because she understands his need to express his feelings of remorse. Further, she appreciates his support and nurturing in the absence of her husband.

The other central male characters in *The Salt Eaters*—James and Fred—share Velma's kind of gender-informed rage and confusion. Espousing white-informed notions of manhood that encourage them to ignore the unique oppressions of women, they displace feelings of social impotence onto their female counterparts. At times this displacement explodes into domestic violence and sexual assault. In most cases, however, it takes on a subtler, but no less debilitating, form—namely, in the ways that black women become ciphers for communal suffering and black male anxieties (sexual, social, and economic). Engaging this displacement as it relates to James's gender crisis, Bambara reveals how even a man who is sympathetic to the plight of black women becomes an active agent in perpetuating sexual abuse by black men.

In "The Construction of O. J. Simpson as a Racial Victim" Devon Carbado underscores the intraracial gender and cultural politics that inform James's gender crisis. In particular, Carbado demonstrates how what he calls the "unmodified antiracist discourse" shapes how most black men process their victimization vis-à-vis that of black women. Carbado asserts that this unmodified antiracist discourse subordinates black gender issues by essentializing racial identity and privileging black male victimhood: "The cumulative racial experiences of Black men are constructed as though they were (1) necessarily inclusive of Black women's experiences and/or (2) deserving of more political attention because such experiences ostensibly indicate that Black men, and not Black women, are endangered. Both of these tendencies create the impression that if we politically and economically 'fix' Black men, we politically and economically 'fix'" Black woman" (168).

This dynamic ensconces the experience of black female oppression in concerns about racial (coded male) oppression. In "'You're Turning Me On': The Boxer, the Beauty Queen, and the Rituals of Gender," Michael Awkward makes the point more forcefully. He argues that this racialized and gendered discourse reinforces the belief that black women, because of their celebrated history of surviving such sexual abuses, should endure the pain of rape and domestic violence "in order to serve the greater good of the race" (13). This pressure to self-sacrifice becomes even more amplified,

Awkward continues, when in highly publicized events, such as the Mike Tyson versus Desirée Washington rape trial, the man is successful, widely celebrated, unassimilated, and perceived as a positive black male role model.

Carbado argues that dismantling the gender taboos that inform such intraracial perspectives is difficult for two primary reasons. First, because stereotyped views of black manhood are—and have been—appropriated to raise social consciousness about issues such as child abuse (Michael Jackson), sexual harassment (Clarence Thomas), rape (Mike Tyson), and spousal abuse (O. J. Simpson). Secondly, because there is a widely (and justifiably) held belief among blacks that the black community is in dire need of positive black male role models. Even though black men can at once be perpetrators of sexual violence against black women *and* victims of a racist justice system, the unmodified antiracist discourse will not allow for such a formulation. Premised as it is on presenting images of black men as "respectable" and "innocent," this discourse treats such acts of black male sexual abuse as inconsequential. Ostensibly, the first (and often only) priority is to eradicate the inequities of the judicial process.

Carbado's theory sheds light on the gender politics that inform James's response to his brother Roland, who has been convicted of brutally raping a black woman. Though James is aware of his brother's guilt, he seriously considers using his political influence to get Roland's conviction overturned. While getting a back massage at the Claybourne community center James reflects, "[M]aybe he could spring Roland and bring him home" (164). Even though James considers lobbying for his brother's freedom, he also appears empathetic toward Roland's victim. Reflecting on her appearance in court, James remarks that she was "huddled on the stand, pinched, nasal, but determined to get justice." He then adds, "She might have been their Aunt Frances, an older sister. She was" (97). Clearly James tries to empathize with the woman by imagining how he would feel if she were a woman he knew and cared for deeply. This gesture appears to show James's sensitivity to the suffering of black women. But a significant question emerges: How can James show genuine empathy for Roland's victim and yet seriously consider getting the conviction overturned?

Closer scrutiny of James's gendered perspective on the suffering of Roland's victim provides some insight into this seeming contradiction. It becomes clear that James's concern for the victim never rises above the kind of unmodified antiracist notion of black female suffering that Carbado identifies. In effect, James's anguish as a traumatized male observer becomes the focal point of his empathy rather than the actual suffering of the woman. This dynamic is evident in the way that James tries to identify with her pain. Rather than imagine how he would feel if he were raped, he imagines how he would feel as a man-protector if a female relative were a rape victim. This gendered point of view is significant because it highlights the limitations of James's empathy. Arguably, James is unable to imagine himself as a rape victim because he privileges his vantage point as a black man over that of a black woman. The emphasis is not on the woman's suffering but on James's imagined suffering as a witness of the rape. In this way, the woman becomes a cipher for black male suffering, making the specificity of her identity and ordeal irrelevant. The way James freely maps other female personas onto her identity attests to this dynamic. Fundamentally, she becomes faceless; her identity as well as her experience of suffering is erased. This erasure is punctuated thematically by the absence of the woman's name and of her perspective on the rape.

The ways in which James identifies with his brother Roland's suffering further illustrate his investment in the unmodified antiracist discourse. James clearly relates to Roland on a much deeper level than he can with the black female rape victim. Bambara brings this connection dramatically into focus when she presents James's response to Roland's letter regarding the rape and his incarceration. Not only is James able to identify with the judicial and penal abuses that his brother outlines in the letter, he is able to "read between the lines" and imagine additional suffering that Roland never outwardly expresses. He observes that the "cramped and scribbly writing . . . was saying other things, about the lame lawyer, the racist judge, the kangeroo [*sic*] court, the vengeful bitch, the rough-off artists in the joint, the lead-pipe shakedowns, the lousy food, the lousy break. No cigarettes, no money, no visitors, no luck, no pussy" (97). James's investment in the unmodified antiracist discourse is unmistakable. Though cognizant of black female suffering, he views black men as the ultimate victims of white oppression. To safeguard black men against the racist abuses of the judicial system, then, takes precedence over addressing the suffering of black women. Though the reader never learns of the final outcome of James's decision regarding Roland, all indications suggest that James will lobby for his freedom.

Bambara amplifies the problematics of this unmodified antiracist discourse in her characterization of Roland. In particular, she shows how Roland's preoccupation with his own social and gender victimization allows him to justify his sexual abuse. He believes, for instance, that no real harm was done to his victim because she was not a virgin at the time of the assault nor has she become pregnant as a result it. Roland's comments to his rape victim during the assault show how he arrives at his disturbing "criteria" for what qualifies as female suffering. He tells his victim, "*Be good to me, bitch, cause no one else has so you take the weight*" (97). Clearly operating from the ideas about black female sacrifice that Awkward outlines, Roland feels that black women should shoulder the "weight" of the black men's social and emotional burdens. Little wonder, then, that Roland fails to consider the emotional suffering of his victim. He views this sacrifice as part of her womanly duty and responsibility to the black (male) community. Since there was no "material" damage incurred by the woman, Roland maintains his innocence, feeling as he does that the woman overreacted.

Though James does not act on his unmodified antiracist thinking in the same violent ways as Roland, his mind-set is no less problematic. Bambara highlights this dynamic by juxtaposing

James's reflections on his brother's crime with his skewed perception of black women as "baby killers." Staring out of the window of the Claybourne community center, James ponders what to do about his brother's dilemma. He then begins to muse on the black biker women below, whom he describes as having "their asses splayed out on the black leather seats" of the motorcycles. He thinks, "Women. Women talking in bits and pieces, mostly waiting, mostly impatient waiting, waiting for the men to straddle the machines and turn on the power and take them somewhere" (99). In his revealingly sexual language, James calls attention to his view of women as powerless, unthinking creatures who depend upon masculine power to give their lives direction and meaning. Even more telling is his charge that his ex-lovers (prior to meeting Velma) were deliberately "killing his babies." James goes so far as to imagine himself as the object of some kind of black female conspiracy to prevent him from fathering a child. He thinks accusingly and sporadically: "Junk food addicts, toxemic pregnancies, miscarriages. Excited mothers-to-be, suddenly sullen and unreachable, terror-stricken, abortions. Pills and foams and curses and shouts and long harangues about you must be kidding you think I'm some fool you sweet talking no dealing or double dealing jive ass drop your seed any ole where and keep stepping and what am I supposed to do kiss my ass and later for all the fucked-up nigger man shit" (99).

Since James exemplifies what Patricia Hill Collins, borrowing from Aretha Franklin, calls a "do right man"—a man who is "faithful, financially reliable, and sexually expressive" to his partner (185)—, it should appear that he would be able to comprehend why a black woman would react negatively to his desire to father a child by her. However, insensitive to the financial and emotional stresses that black women have incurred from deadbeat boyfriends, husbands, and fathers, James depicts black women as if they are pathologically uncaring and hostile to the struggles of black men. For him, the "pattern is clear" (99). Ultimately, it takes Velma—who is also unable to bear him a child—to raise his political consciousness. When he tells her his female conspiracy thesis, she winces and asks, "What kind of poor, abused sistuh would want to kill your baby, James?" (99). Even though James acknowledges that Velma's comment helped him to "foster a new pattern of growth" regarding black female issues, the reader questions his sincerity; it is not long after his musing that he contemplates lobbying for Roland's release from prison.

Bambara further explores the problematic ways in which black men conceptualize their victimization in her rendering of the black bus driver Fred Holt. Specifically, she explores the impact of what she calls "false white identity" on the construction of black masculinity. In an interview with Kalamu ya Salaam, Bambara uses a spatial metaphor to describe the ideological and cultural dilemmas her characters confront. She observes that blacks "invest too much time looking at how they are boxed in on all four sides [so that] they never look up and know that they can build upwards. To constantly be looking at those four sides is to stay in prison, is to collaborate with your captors, indeed, is to lend them energy, which is the same thing as providing them with the power to keep you locked in" (51). The "four sides" of Fred Holt's ideological and cultural "prison" are dramatically displayed in the way he fetishizes his white wife. Exposing the unacknowledged racial motives that undergird his decision to marry a white woman, Fred explains that he married Margie to "reward himself with blond hair" after his first black wife left him to join a black nationalist group. Ideology clashes with reality when he does not receive the rewards—social, emotional, or sexual—that he anticipates. Though Fred lists Margie's poor domestic skills as the primary cause of his resentment toward her, it becomes apparent that her inability to identify with his suffering as a black man lies at the core of his angst. When, in a fit of rage, Fred runs over a raccoon in the street, he muses on his wife's response: "And of course when he got home tonight, he could count on her to ask him the same dumb thing: 'have a nice trip, Freddie?' No sleep, brains cooked, lousy meals, the worse shift, Porter dead, uniform a mess, so she had it coming. 'I ran over a coon. As in raccoon. Not to be confused with the coons your daddy used to lynch.' And she'd cry. Not *for him*, not for his chafed neck and his jounced nuts, his loss, his threatened pension. But for herself and some dead animal" (84; my emphasis).

Blind to the ideology that motivated him to marry a white woman in the first place, Fred imagines that his wife's sexual and emotional inattentiveness toward him is the result of her racial superiority complex. Though he is primarily responsible for putting her on a pedestal, he constructs his relationship with her as though she deliberately uses her whiteness to undermine him. He likens her to a prostitute who thinks her whiteness alone licenses her to treat him like a subordinate. He thinks, "Margie. With her streaked and stringy hair and flat ass acting like she was some kind of movie star, prancing about the house in her drawers. Giving him her back at night like he was supposed to be grateful for whatever she offered" (79). Ironically, Fred highlights her physical features as negative attributes, the same features, like "blond hair," that he ostensibly identifies as drawing him to her initially. Fred's central dilemma lies not with his "unloving" white wife, but in his own belief that her "whiteness" somehow makes her a more viable and "valuable" partner than a black woman. That Fred acknowledges that he couldn't talk with Porter about his white wife because he was a race man exhibits that, on some conscious level, he is aware of how his decision to marry a white woman would be perceived. However, rather than addressing the problematics of his own ideology—that to marry a white woman is somehow a step-up on the social scale—he displaces the blame and responsibility onto his wife. At bottom, he resents his wife for lacking a characteristic that, because of her whiteness, she is incapable of having—the ability to empathize with him from the standpoint of a black woman who experiences a similar kind of racial oppression. Scapegoating Margie for his unhappiness allows Fred to evade responsibility for his personal stake in reinforcing racial hierarchies.

Bambara calls attention to the contradictions in Fred Holt's value system by invoking Ralph Ellison's essay "Change the Joke and Slip the Yoke." Direct references to the idea of the racial "joke" discussed in his essay are vividly displayed in Porter's advice to Fred regarding racial invisibility. Porter refers directly to Ellison when he says, "They [white people] call the Black man The Invisible Man. And that becomes a double joke and then a double cross then a triple funny all around. Our natures are unknowable, unseeable to them. They haven't got the eyes for us. Course, when we look at us with their eyes, we disappear, ya know?" (159). Similarly, in "Change the Joke and Slip the Yoke" Ellison observes, "The white man's half-conscious awareness that his image of the Negro is false makes him suspect the Negro of always seeking to take him in, and assume his motives are anger and fear—which very often they are. On his side of the joke the Negro looks at the white man and finds it difficult to believe that . . . [he] can be so absurdly self-deluded over the true interrelatedness of blackness and whiteness. To him the white man seems a hypocrite who boasts of a pure identity while standing with his humanity exposed to the world" (55).

Ostensibly, Ellison shows that even as whites are aware that their image of blacks is mostly false, they nevertheless embrace this image because of their own anxieties about white identity. Ellison's aim is to demonstrate that masking is not a unique African American practice created in response to white oppression. Rather, it is an American practice that cuts across racial lines. To illustrate his point, he shows how prominent white men such as Benjamin Franklin, Abraham Lincoln, William Faulkner, and Ernest Hemingway donned social masks as "average men" to disguise their intelligence and bolster their respective careers. Black masking, Ellison argues, is no less complex. It is not motivated by fear of white oppression so much as by a "profound rejection of the image created [by whites] to usurp . . . [black] identity. Sometimes it is for the sheer joy of the joke; sometimes to challenge those who presume, across the psychological distance created by race manners, to know . . . [black] identity" (55).

At once drawing upon and revising Ellison's notion of the joke so that it better accounts for the gross inequities in power, Bambara has Porter present Ellison's argument to Fred. The "double funny" to which Porter refers above can be read as whites' inability to construct real, paradoxical images of themselves and blacks. This false consciousness is a "double cross" for blacks because such a warped perspective works to the ultimate disadvantage—social, political, and economic—of blacks in a white-dominated society. The "triple funny" is that blacks have internalized this warped perspective of blackness to such an extent that they see themselves as racially inferior. Porter says, "[W]hen we look at us with their eyes, we disappear" (159). Thus for blacks to see themselves through the eyes of their oppressors is to erase the richness and complexity of their individual consciousnesses and their collective cultural ethos. Getting in tune with one's cultural spirit, Porter explains, is "not just looking different . . . but being different. Your true nature [is] invisible because you're in some incongruous getup or in some incongruous place or the looker's got incongruous eyes" (159).

It is with "their eyes" that Fred interprets his own situation with his wife and, concomitantly, Porter's advice about the Transchemical Company (read: white male social dominance) that buries its hazardous wastes in the black community. When Porter explains to Fred how the Transchemical Company will probably try to destroy the town's infirmary because there are "too many [black educated] agitator types over there" who are probably "collecting information about conditions at the plant, [and] its effect on our lungs," Fred misinterprets his advocacy for the infirmary as a warning to stay away from it (71). The narrator records his response: "And Fred had stared out the diner window towards the building [infirmary] he'd been meaning to go by for the longest for a checkup. But not if agitators hung around there. He'd had enough trouble in life" (71).

Ironically, after Porter dies, Fred diagnoses his own cultural dilemma when he tries to cross over a mud puddle occupied by thirsty pigeons in order to strike up a conversation with a boy (Velma and James's adopted son) who reminds him of his own son as a teenager. When the pigeons refuse to relinquish their position and wind up splashing Fred's pants and shoes with muddy water, he reflects: "So used to dipping your beaks in muddy water and turpentine, [you] wouldn't know what to do at a fresh lake spring if you got a paid vacation" (155). Analogous to the single-minded pigeons, Fred has spent his entire life wallowing in a self-deprecating ideology. Confounded by his own internalized notions of white superiority, he can no longer distinguish between his own views of his personhood/manhood and the identity assigned to him by the dominant culture. Little wonder, then, that Fred cannot fully perceive of his "blackness" as redeeming or empowering despite Porter's cultural insights; he has become accustomed to evaluating his cultural identity by the standards of white society.

Though not fully drawn, the process of Fred's cultural healing begins at the infirmary, where, in a dreamlike state, he reencounters Porter. Mute and unaware of Fred's presence, Porter exhibits what Fred perceives as a nonchalant attitude that recalls his shifting outlook during the days before his death. Fred reflects on how, during those final days, Porter no longer put stock in the small civil rights gains that helped him to secure a spot on the dayshift, his apartment lease, and the like. He observes that Porter was acting as if he were "preparing himself for a new life" (280). What he perceives as Porter's emotional detachment can be read as his break from the ideological and political binds of the white status quo. Recognizing that the "things so hard won" by the civil rights movement were more symbolic than real representations of racial progress, Porter abandons his investment in the "American Dream" and begins the process of cultural recovery and self-actualization. After studying briefly with the Hermit (Cleotus)—a male version of Minnie Ransom—Porter tells Fred, "Ain't no graduates from the university I study at" (159). Put simply, white society will not sanction or reward radical cultural thinking and action that challenges its racially coded principles. Porter's ghostly appearance at the infirmary recalls and reflects his advice to Fred that once an individual comprehends his "true nature" he doesn't just "look different," he becomes "different."

Though Fred doesn't fully comprehend Porter's advice, his eventual decision to get a checkup at the infirmary and to arrange a meeting with Minnie Ransom suggests that he is headed in the right direction. After he accidentally walks in during the last stages of Velma's healing process and receives such strong and positive vibes from the people congregated around her, he remarks ironically, and somewhat humorously, "There was no one who looked like agitators or troublemakers to him. Porter had probably gotten that all wrong" (270–71). Though Fred misreads Porter's initial advice regarding the workers at the infirmary, he somehow manages to find his way back to the cultural storehouse. Remarking on his healing process in the interview with Kalamu ya Salaam, Bambara notes that, though Fred is culturally "off-center," there "have been enough people in his life to . . . spin him back" toward the right direction (51).

A more complete understanding of the male identity crisis in *The Salt Eaters* brings the interlocking politics that perpetuate antagonisms between black men and women into focus. In particular, it reveals how physical and psychological coping mechanisms employed by blacks since slavery to protect themselves against the constant threat of white terrorism have, in many cases, forestalled the possibility of cultural healing. Certainly, both during and after the antebellum era blacks have had to think and perceive of reality like their white oppressors did in order to root out any behavior that might invoke white wrath. These coping strategies, however, have also fostered a self-policing and self-critical environment wherein blacks turn against each other to vent their social rage, a phenomenon that inadvertently reifies the status quo. Convinced, like Fred, that white social and cultural dominance is an inevitability of American life, many blacks chose to blame whites, assertive black women, or abusive black men for their personal unhappiness rather than, as Bambara proposes, seeking out culturally specific ways to empower themselves and their communities. As demonstrated, even cultural warriors like Velma and James, who have dedicated most of their lives to fighting for black liberation, are deeply implicated in this "blame game."

Invoking folk wisdom in "What It Is I Think I'm Doing Anyhow," Bambara asserts that "It's not how little we know that hurts so, but that so much of what we know ain't so" (155). In regard to gender issues, Bambara demonstrates what "ain't so" about the reality of white and male oppression. She shows how many blacks become unwitting agents in maintaining and perpetuating their own racial, gender, and cultural subjugation. The novel suggests that identifying and acknowledging the extent of one's complicity can open up new and effective possibilities for liberation. Sophie speaks directly to this issue when she asserts that blacks need to "[k]eep the focus on the action not the institution" and be careful not to "confuse the vehicle with the objective" (199). To this end, contesting and interrogating the ideology of racial and gender privilege becomes a more productive political endeavor than casting whites and men as perpetual victimizers. Indeed, eschewing the temptation to assign blame is difficult, given the intensity and frequency in which blacks generally, and black women in particular, experience oppression. However, as Bambara has shown, the marked advantage to maintaining a wider, more visionary perspective is that it allows the individual to recognize his or her ability to transform self, community, and society. To recognize that, despite the overwhelming disparities in power, one has options and choices is integral to ushering in a new era of black liberation generally, and ameliorating the relationship between black men and women specifically. The narrator reports that during the storm at the end of the novel, "[c]hoices were being tossed into the street like dice . . . shells . . . kola nuts [and] . . . jackstones" (94). For Bambara, it is not a question of whether black Americans have the power to transform social and personal realities, but whether they can identify and tap into their cultural powers in order to do so. As Minnie relays plainly and profoundly to Velma, you "[a]lways got options" (44).

5

"LIKE A BUTTERFLY IN A HURRICANE": RECONCEPTUALIZING BLACK GENDERED RESISTANCE IN WALTER MOSLEY'S *ALWAYS OUTNUMBERED, ALWAYS OUTGUNNED* AND *WALKIN' THE DOG*

IN A CRUCIAL SCENE in Walter Mosley's *Always Outnumbered, Always Outgunned* Socrates Fortlow, an ex-con who has been to prison for over thirty years for double homicide and rape, leads a small group of men in deciding how to deal with a junkie in their community, Petis, who has resorted to killing people for drug money. Socrates must negotiate between two opposing options that emerge from the group. His best friend Right thinks that they should kill Petis, while Markham, a local resident, thinks that they should turn the matter over to the police. Neither option appeals to Socrates because the first involves killing another black man and the second involves placing faith in a racially biased judicial system. Trying to avoid these pitfalls, Socrates convinces the men to run Petis out of their community by force. Though they are successful in getting Petis to leave (primarily because of a severe beating Socrates gives him), Socrates remains conflicted about whether they succeeded in promoting any positive change in the community, because Petis is ultimately killed as a result of having been forced out of their neighborhood. When one of the participants in the vigilante action suggests that the men become a permanent policing force in the community "because it worked out [so] good the first time," Socrates responds distraughtly, "We ain't some kinda gangbangers, man. We cain't live like that. We did what we had to do. But you know, I don't know if I'd have the heart ever to do it again" (36).

Several questions of profound significance to a black male feminist critique emerge from this scene: How does Socrates's cultural and gendered perspective on the police complicate his decision regarding Petis? Why is Socrates conflicted about the outcome of the group's vigilante action? Why does he associate their efforts to make their community safer with gangbanging? And, most crucially, how do Socrates's notions of black manhood inform the way he views his involvement in Petis's death?

While *Always Outnumbered* brings these questions into focus, Mosley pursues them much further toward their resolution in *Walkin' the Dog*. In the most pivotal scene in the novel, Socrates facilitates an intense gender debate within his discussion group over which gender suffers more, a debate he generates in part by asking the group whether they should hold whites or themselves responsible for the many problems that plague the black community. As tensions reach a head, Socrates tells a story about a group of slave rebels who kill their slave owners, escape to nearby hills, and wage war against the local slave-holding community. The political plight of the slave rebels is sullied, Socrates implies, because in killing their slave owners the rebels severely compromise their own spiritual beliefs. Failing to come to terms with the guilt they feel for compromising these beliefs, the rebels displace their anxieties on to other blacks, killing those who refuse to join their ranks.

Socrates's story radically changes the tenor of the gender debate. The focus of the discussion shifts to trying to understand why the slave rebels reacted to their oppression in such destructive ways. This new dialogue generates several important questions about black suffering: Why did the slaves choose to stay and fight rather than escape to freedom? Why did they betray their moral and spiritual beliefs about murder? And, finally, why did they kill blacks who refused to join their ranks? The group's new focus is significant because rather than defending their right to blame whites or each other for black suffering, they begin to investigate the complexity of blame and suffering across racial and gender lines. Such a focus clears the pathway for a more rigorous and useful approach to critiquing intraracial gender and cultural dilemmas.

I conclude *Breaking the Silence* with a discussion of Mosley because he provides a black male feminist framework in *Always Outnumbered, Always Outgunned* and *Walkin' the Dog* for moving beyond the gendered obstacles identified in Himes, Baldwin, Morrison, and Bambara. This framework illuminates the disjuncture between the theory and practice of black resistance, demonstrating the need to construct new models of gender and resistance that are conducive to the emotional, cultural, and psychological well-being of the black community. As my previous chapters reveal, failure to construct these new gender and resistance models (or, at least, to recognize the need to invent new ones) has dire social and cultural consequences. Unaware of the inherent problems of their gender and resistance models, blacks impose unrealistic social demands on each other (and whites) that ultimately lead to unproductive scapegoating. This scapegoating, in turn, fosters social resignation rather than empowerment because it obscures blacks' ability to fully comprehend their social agency. Mosley reveals that moving beyond this social resignation requires that blacks come to terms with how they participate, directly and indirectly, in the maintenance of the status quo and the concomitant disintegration of the black community. Such awareness is necessary in order to invent new and effective resistance strategies.

In "Giving Back," Mosley's signature essay in the black self-help anthology *Black Genius,* he introduces a resistance strategy for blacks that brings his cultural vision in *Always Outnumbered* and *Walkin' the Dog* into focus. He argues that the anger blacks harbor toward whites stifles black social and economic potential. Complicated by emotional and psychological dependency on white philanthropy and goodwill, this anger makes it difficult for blacks to distinguish the oppressor from the ideology of oppression. This distinction is critical, as feminist scholar Deirdre Lashgari notes, in "To Speak the Unspeakable: Implications of Gender, 'Race,' Class, and Culture," because any form of victimized anger that is aimed at the perpetrator rather than at the system of oppression "merely replicates the problem" of oppression (9). As both Toni Morrison and Toni Cade Bambara demonstrate, the ideological system that creates and sustains the oppressive mind-set remains intact. Cognizant of this ideological pitfall, Mosley structures his resistance strategy on self and cultural love rather than on black anger. To move beyond the impasse of anger, blacks need to do more than revise resistance strategies generated within binary structures of black/white, victimized/victimizer. They have to create frameworks that address the multiple, complex social realities of black folk.

To create these new modes of resistance, Mosley asserts, blacks must avoid mythologizing and romanticizing their shared legacy of oppression. He writes, "If we . . . love each other and . . . our race, then we have to be critical of ourselves and honest. We don't need charity or self-pity or defense" (48). Mosley surmises that many blacks will be angered by this rigorously self-reflective approach because it requires them to recognize their complicity in black oppression, on the one hand, and to let go of their justifiable anger and resentment of whites, on the other: "We can't support the men and women who say that the white man is too much for them. We have to say, 'No, sister. No, brother. You're wrong about that. You've got the power in your hands.' There's love in that phrase, but many people will be angry when you say it. Angry because we have lived through many generations in which white America has done its best to disable our love for ourselves. The expectations of love are too much for many of us. It's easier to share the feeling of defeat; the false blues" (49).

To suggest that white oppression is too formidable an obstacle for blacks to overcome is to concede that blacks have no control over their social and economic circumstances. Mosley vehemently rejects this kind of cultural thinking because it inadvertently reifies white supremacy, implying that the social fate of blacks is predetermined by race. His rejection of this kind of cultural thinking as the "false blues" highlights its cultural and political bankruptcy.

To fully appreciate Mosley's reference to the blues, one has to understand how the blues functions as a mode of black resistance. Expounding on this function in *Daughters: On Family and Fatherhood,* Gerald Early writes poignantly:

> Perhaps, I love them [the blues] because the attitude toward life expressed in blues records—that everyone has troubles but they can be endured, that happiness is not lasting, so don't be fooled by your good times—is truly the essence of "blackness." Blues don't promise that people will not be unhappy, but that unhappiness can be transcended, not by faith in God, but by faith in one's own ability to accept unhappiness without ever conceding oneself to it. Blackness is not an Afrocentric lesson, nor a coming together of the tribe in fake unity. It is this: a fatalistic, realistic belief in human transcendence, born in the consciousness of a people who experienced the gutwrenching harshness of slavery, of absorbing the absolute annihilation of their humanity, and who lived to tell the world and their former masters about it. And it is about how they reinvented their humanity in the meanwhile. (143–44)

Read against Early's insightful delineation of blues politics, to have the "false blues" is to believe that harboring resentment toward whites is the only real recourse for blacks in a white supremacist world. This perspective is "false" precisely because it erases black social agency; suffering becomes an end in itself rather than a testimony to the dogged fortitude of blacks who refused—and refuse— to allow white oppression to dictate the course of their lives.

For Mosley, then, examining how black anger produces this "false blues" is crucial to black empowerment. Ultimately, he believes that if blacks are to alter their debilitating social and economic circumstances they must do so by identifying and eliminating their complicity in oppression. This emphasis on complicity does not absolve whites of their responsibility for creating and perpetuating black oppression. Rather it addresses the reality of black-white race relations in America, emphasizing that in order for blacks to make any type of social or economic gains they must unfairly shoulder the burden of altering their own racial realities.

Always Outnumbered is structured thematically and stylistically as a short story cycle, rather than a disconnected collection of related short stories. Crediting James Joyce with revolutionizing how contemporary collections of short stories are structured and read, Craig Werner notes, "Prior to [Joyce's] *Dubliners,* short story volumes were, with few exceptions, collections of random pieces. Since *Dubliners,* many have instead sought the unity long associated with the best volumes of poetry" (35). Joyce's text, Werner continues, "provides three basic techniques for unifying story cycles; (1) focusing on one well-defined setting . . . ; (2) developing a group of central thematic issues from different perspectives . . . ; and (3) manipulating narrative stance to reflect shifting authorial attitude toward the subject matter" (35). Set in Los Angeles during the 1980s and narrated by Socrates Fortlow at different stages of his cultural and intellectual development, *Always Outnumbered* meets at least two of the criteria for a unified story cycle that Werner outlines. In fact, so fluid and intersecting are the stories in *Always Outnumbered* that many readers mistake it for a novel.

In his rendering of the relationship between Socrates and his mentee Darryl in the opening scene in *Always Outnumbered,* Mosley illuminates the link between cultural responsibility and black manhood. This relationship is important to Mosley's political schema in that it challenges white notions of black male criminality, on one hand, while deromanticizing notions of "gangsta" life on the other. Socrates is not a hardened criminal who lacks remorse for those he has unjustly killed. But neither is he a fully reformed ex-con, reconciled to the problems of his former life. His mentorship of Darryl reflects his complex character; rather than teach Darryl an abstract distinction between "right" and "wrong" (a distinction that often perplexes Socrates), he tries to get Darryl to recognize that in order to be a man he must become aware of how his actions, positive and negative, impact the larger black community.

Socrates's first encounter with Darryl brings Mosley's cultural and gender politics into focus. He apprehends Darryl for killing and trying to steal his neighbor's pet rooster. In interrogating Darryl's motives, Socrates discovers that he has murdered another boy. Rather than condemn Darryl, however, Socrates attempts to educate him about the far-reaching emotional, cultural, and social effects of his actions. Aware that Darryl's street/survivalist mentality sanctions his senseless act of violence, Socrates tries to get him to view his victim as more than just a causality of the streets. He does so by forcing the boy to clean and prepare the rooster that he has killed, an exercise intended to teach him to take responsibility for his actions. Underscoring this responsibility, Socrates tells Darryl to make sure he "rinse[s] out all the [rooster's] blood" because a "[m]an could get sick on blood" (16). Clearly, the metaphoric language invokes the need for Darryl to come to terms with and attempt to rectify the "blood" that is on his hands regarding the boy he has murdered. Most important, however, it highlights the link between manhood and cultural responsibility that undergirds Socrates's and Mosley's political strategy.

Socrates's advice to Darryl on how to atone for his crimes underscores one of the central political themes of the novel: that black men need to revise their ideas about black manhood to deal with the complex and mutable dynamics of institutional racism in America. Close scrutiny of Socrates's conversation with Darryl reveals the complications inherent in this process of gender revision. When Darryl informs Socrates that regardless of the circumstances, "I ain't goin' t' no fuckin' jail" (22), Socrates explains to him that accepting responsibility for his actions does not necessarily mean that he should turn himself into the police. Serving prison time, Socrates informs him, will not erase or rectify his crimes. "I don't blame you" for not wanting to go to prison, he says. "Jail ain't gonna help a damn thing. Better shoot yo'self than got to jail" (22). Socrates continues, "We all got to be our own judge, lil brother. 'Cause if you don't know when you wrong then yo' life ain't worf a damn" (23).

On first glance, Socrates's advice might seem unethical and irresponsible. When his advice is distilled, however, it becomes clear that there is a much more complex moral and ethical dynamic at work. To fully appreciate Socrates's perspective, the reader must consider his advice in relation to the social and economic variables that shape the realities of poor, urban black men. As Mosley explains in an interview with Peter Hogness, "the moral template of our larger society . . . doesn't fit [the world in which] he [Socrates] lives. So he has to re-create one that does, the same way that black people are always recreating our own lives" (4). Having been incarcerated for more than half his life, Socrates understands how the penal system can further harden convicted felons. Forced to endure gross racist abuse, black prisoners often fail to come to terms with the crimes that they committed. In effect, their unfair treatment serves to overshadow their crimes. Recognizing that going to prison will not ensure that Darryl will understand the severity of crimes (that, indeed, it might harden him even further), Socrates presents Darryl with another alternative that may possibly raise his consciousness. Though his alternative is certainly not fail-safe, it provides Darryl with a better opportunity to come to grips with his crimes than sending him to prison would.

Socrates aids Darryl in his rehabilitation process by helping him to understand how his crimes, particularly those against other blacks, operate to sustain what I call "implosive victimization"— the psychological process by which rage and despair are systematically turned against the victimized. Socrates elucidates this process when he takes Darryl to visit Right Burke, who lives in one of the poorest and most crime-ridden areas in the city. Working in tandem with Right, Socrates shows Darryl how the police officers, particularly black ones, operate as enforcers of the white status quo in impoverished black urban centers. Specifically, Socrates shows him how this policing effort directly and indirectly encourages blacks to abuse one another.

Calling Darryl's attention to a house that the police use as a surveillance point to monitor the activities of a black radical organization, the Young Africans, Socrates points out the irony of how the police department, comprised of both whites and blacks, allocates exorbitant energy and resources to spy on a group whose ultimate aim is to empower and liberate black people, while numerous crimes occur in the community literally in front of their faces. Socrates observes half-jokingly that the police are probably worried about the Young Africans' making bombs or, "even worse," that they will get "all the other Negroes to vote" (84). He further points out that while the black cops are busy spying on the college students, Darryl's best friend Jamal "is right down the street gettin' his dick suck[ed]" and a crack house is in full operation "almost next do'" (88–89). To punctuate his observations to Darryl, he asks rhetorically, "Do that sound like the law to you . . .?" (88). Riffing off Socrates, Right Burke (whose name clearly invokes the black "rights" that are being undermined by both the whites in power and the black policemen who enforce the status quo) calls Darryl's attention to the economic implications of the police stakeout. In particular, he explains how the money invested in this policing effort could be used more productively to assist the poor and elderly in the black community. Addressing his own socioeconomic circumstances, Right points out that the makeshift black nursing home in which he lives is supported primarily by the few donations that Luvia, the landlady, manages to procure from local church and civic organizations. It is ironic and tragic, Right observes, that the city will pay nearly twenty-five hundred dollars a day to monitor "some kids" when "you got twenty old people right here" at the nursing home who can "hardly pay for food" (88).

While Socrates and Right call Darryl's attention to the social and political forces that attempt to thwart the efforts of radical black activists groups like the Young Africans, neither endorses such groups as the means by which blacks will acquire liberation. Socrates openly questions their black nationalist politics, drawing attention to how they are disconnected from the lives, consciousness, and realities of those they ostensibly champion. He tells Darryl that though he appreciates their liberating, pro-black rhetoric, "words ain't deeds": "You don't teach people, you love 'em. You don't get a house and a printin' press and put up a fence. You do like Luvia. You open up your arms and your pocketbook" (91).

As Socrates's mentorship of Darryl shows, it is clear that he is not condemning efforts to educate the black masses. Rather he is critiquing the abstractionism and militancy that underlies the Young Africans' political ideology. Additionally, he calls attention to the problems that adhere to political movements that fail to consider the material and emotional needs and concerns of their constituencies. Socrates observes that "The Young Africans [are] like a gang. They got their code an' their colors. They ready to go to war. An' that's fine. Sometimes you got to war. But most of the times you should be helpin'. You should be laughin' an' eatin' good an' you should go to bed knowin' that they ain't nobody hungry on yo' street"(91).

To break the cycle of oppression and poverty, Socrates implies, blacks must reassess their racial and social priorities. Above all, they must take responsibility for ensuring the financial, emotional, and spiritual stability of their communities. All else is secondary. His political argument follows this line of reasoning: It is foolish to devote so many valuable resources to usurping the power of the oppressor (a strategy that has only generated minimal political gains in the past), when those same resources could be used to help house, feed, and educate blacks who need immediate assistance. Socrates underscores this sentiment when he tells Darryl that even though "[c]ops don't mean shit"—regardless of their authority, they cannot ultimately dictate his or the black community's behavior—the black community cannot "let . . . [a] crack house be on [their] . . . street neither" (91). Similarly, blacks cannot allow people to starve or remain homeless in their communities, regardless of what whites do or do not do.

Mosley illustrates this approach to resistance in his portrait of the black-owned-and-operated Capricorn bookstore that Socrates frequents during the crucial months following his release from prison. The culturally supportive environment the bookstore provides is particularly critical for Socrates, who left prison full of anger, resentment, and rage. During his first days of freedom, "[h]e was waiting for somebody to give him a look so he could break their face for them" (154). However, acting as a kind of therapy, his interactions and conversations with other intelligent and conscientious blacks at the bookstore helped him come to terms with and identify his unintentional complicity in black oppression. He articulates his revelation to the owners of the bookstore, Mr. and Mrs. Minette, while dining with them in their apartment. Rejecting their well-intentioned claim that by serving his prison sentence he had fully repaid his debt to society, he responds thoughtfully, "I got out [of prison] okay, but you know I was mean then too. They let me go 'cause all I did was kill black folks. They don't think that black folks are worth a whole life in a white man's jail. But I wasn't cured. I was still mean an' still confused. You know my main problem was that I was never quite sure what was right. You know—absolutely sure" (162). (Mis)interpreting Socrates's delineation of "implosive victimization" (and his active participation in it) as a defeatist and spiritually bankrupt approach to resistance, Mr. Minette tries to convince him that "he is a good man" because, unlike most people, "you know, in your heart, that there's something good in the world in spite of all the bad you've seen and been" (162). He tells Socrates that he is part of a "divine plan" and that the insights that he has gained from his struggles in this life will move him closer to some higher calling. "There's a high sign," Mr. Minette asserts, "but not everybody can see it. But you saw it" (163).

Though flattered by Mr. Minette's perception of him as ultimately good, Socrates rejects the notion of a divine plan. Its teleological premise—we are all moving linearly toward a greater good—obscures the systematic and institutionalized cycle of blacks venting their oppressive rage onto each other. Socrates responds respectfully, "I wanna believe you. And I sure don't wanna make you mad. But there ain't no plan. No sir there ain't. There's rules; all kinda rules. And rules is always made to put money in another man's pocket; food in somebody else's children's mouths" (163). He further notes that "any black man that ever did a thing for hisself broke the rules—he had to because the rules say that a black man can't have nuthin'" (163). Having played by the rules of the white supremacist game, Socrates recognizes that he has been an active agent in his and the black community's destruction. He believes Mr. and Mrs. Minette are the real revolutionaries because they "broke the rules" by creating the space for blacks to come together to address their issues. He tells them, "You started that store, made room for black men and women, and didn't take no collection and didn't tell 'em what to think. You had me here to dinner an' opened your heart. That's revolution, brother, rebellion against the rule" (164).

Referring to his own complicity, Socrates notes that he inadvertently "played by the rules" by targeting other blacks, contributing ultimately to the social devaluation of black life. If justice had been properly served, he says, then he would have been "hung, gassed, and then electrocuted" for his brutal crimes. Because he only murdered other blacks, however, white society "rewarded" him with life and eventual freedom. Socrates reflects, "That was the trick for me. I thought I knew what I was doin' but I was just workin' for the men made the rules. Killin' my own people was just part 'a the rules. Makin' myself a jailbird was just what they wanted" (164).

Here, Socrates lays out another aspect of "implosive victimization"—namely, the ways that the judicial system creates and promotes internal strife and bloodshed by directly and indirectly encouraging black-on-black homicide. This process of "implosive victimization" is most clearly evident in the ways the police judicial system metes out longer jail sentences for black-on-white homicide than for black-on-black homicide. This racially coded sentencing process, literally and figuratively, creates a cycle of oppression that rewards black men for killing each other. Poor, undereducated, and economically disenfranchised, the majority of these black offenders, when paroled, return to the same socioeconomic conditions that fostered their crimes in the first instance. In most cases they either kill again or get killed. The systemic perpetuation of this cycle ultimately reinforces the notion that black lives are less valuable than those of whites.

Discussing the L.A. Riots and the subsequent burning down of the Capricorn bookstore with Roland, a former patron, Socrates addresses how even race riots assure the maintenance and perpetuation of implosive victimization. Meditating on the cultural mind-set that provokes such mass violence and destruction, he informs Roland that he understands why black men feel that they are rebelling against the white mainstream by burning down the city. "It feels like rebellion," Socrates observes. "Like a prison riot—men fightin' for their freedom. That always feels like a revolution. But you know, you burn down your own home in the face 'a the enemy an' it's just followin' his rule: doin' what he want you to" (167). As Socrates knows, these poor black men express their outrage through rioting because they want to show their oppressors that they cannot be ignored or taken lightly.

Using violence to combat violence, however, substantiates rather than challenges the ways that whites have historically controlled blacks. By expressing their social frustration in this way, black men inadvertently reify the constellation out of which white supremacy is created and sustained. In effect, they justify the use of violence against them. To this end, they follow rather than break "the rules" of white oppression. Ultimately, their reckless abandon assists in further fracturing and dividing their communities. Underscoring this point to Roland, Socrates says, "I wanted to loot and burn. I wanted to firebomb a police car an' then take their guns an' shoot down helicopters. But them helicopters woulda crashed in my own people's homes, an' they woulda killed a hunnert innocent Negroes just to bring me down" (167).

Socrates's delineation of implosive victimization recalls Ernest Gaines's short story "Three Men," in which an older black convict delineates the relation between manhood and complicity. Munford—who has been allowed to murder and assault other black men with impunity because of his father's affiliation with a prominent white man in the community—tries to warn the much younger Procter, who has committed his first murder against a black man, not to fall prey to the emasculating process of white philanthropy. Relaying his personal history to Procter, Munford explains, "Been going in and out of these jails here, I don't know how long . . . Forty, fifty years. Started out just like you—kilt a boy just like you did last night. Kilt him and got off—got off scot-free. My pappy worked for a white man who got me off. At first I didn't know why he had done it—I didn't think; all I know was I was free, and free is how I wanted to be" (135). Munford then observes, "I got in trouble again, and again they got me off. I kept on getting in trouble, and they kept on getting me off. Didn't wake up till I got to be nearly old as I'm is now. Then I realized they kept getting me off because they [white men] needed a Munford Bazille. They need me to prove they human—just like they need that thing over there. They need us" (135). Illuminating the link between black crime and white manhood, Munford calls attention to how he was used, directly and indirectly, by his white "benefactor" to secure the notion of white men's moral and masculine superiority over black men. By playing the role of "bad nigger"—recklessly killing other black men—he unintentionally reifies the man/boy, civilized/primitive binaries used to sustain white male superiority and to emasculate black men.

Socially, these binaries were visible (particularly during the Jim Crow era) in the ways that white men would refer to black men as "boys" and "children," while demanding by force and law that black men refer to them with deferential titles such as "mister," "master," and "boss." Such institutional practices reinforced paternalistic notions that white men were the moral and physical "guardians" of black people. Without this white guardianship, the thinking went, blacks would perish in a "civilized" society, unequipped as they were by nature to survive on their own. Little wonder, then, that Munford's white overseer continues to bail him

out of jail. Recklessly killing other black men, Munford legitimates white arguments regarding black brutality, immorality, and
savagery. Releasing him back onto the streets benefits his overseer
and white men in at least two ways: they gain moral and social
currency for their supposed philanthropy, while simultaneously
ensuring the maintenance of the status quo vis-à-vis the reinforce-
ment of these racial binaries. That Munford continues to accept
these offers of "freedom" makes him an active agent in advancing
the aims of white supremacy.

Having become aware of how his violence against other blacks
contributes to the maintenance of the status quo, Munford advises
Procter not to accept the offer of "freedom" that will inevitably be
made to him by his white overseer Roger Medlow. Munford warns
Procter that if he allows Medlow to bail him out of jail, he will
become a co-conspirator in his and the black community's social
and cultural undoing. Munford explains that "they grow niggers
just to be killed, and they grow people like you to kill 'em. That's
all part of . . . the culture. And every man got to play his part in
the culture, or the culture don't go on" (142). The only way for
Procter to disrupt this "culture" is to refuse to accept his role in
the man/boy, civilized/primitive binary, a decision that at best will
get him a long prison sentence and at worst get him killed. Such
an act of resistance is dangerous because it casts light on the subversive policing element that underpins the white men's offers of
freedom, revealing the myriad ways that whites benefit from and
promote this cycle of oppression. White philanthropy gets revealed
as a veiled effort to maintain the status quo. Paradoxically, then,
Procter can affirm his humanity and manhood only if he accepts
imprisonment or death as the requisite cost of his and the black
community's liberation. Munford underscores this paradox when
he responds to Procter's fear that Medlow will have him murdered
within a month in prison if he rejects his offer of clemency. If you
are killed, Munford says, "At least you [would have] been a man
a month—where if you let him get you out you won't be a man a
second. He won't 'low it" (341).

Though the reader never learns of Procter's ultimate fate (or that of Munford, who, ironically, is released from prison on his own recognizance), it is clear that in order for Procter to carry through with Munford's advice he must come to terms with, and ultimately take responsibility for, the fact that his actions, positive or negative, have a major impact on the black community. The process of his political and cultural development is dramatically displayed when a black boy, severely beaten for theft, is thrown into the cell with him and Hattie, a homosexual prostitute. When Hattie begins to comfort the young boy in a sexually seductive manner, Procter becomes incensed and takes the boy away from him. Though Procter's actions can certainly be read as homophobic, they also can be read as his attempt to prevent the boy (and himself) from falling prey to the "prostitution" of black manhood, symbolic and literal, that has ensnared Munford and Hattie. In effect, Procter is preparing the boy and, to a large extent, himself to break this cycle of prostitution/oppression. Procter realizes that in order for him to endure the beating or death that will inevitably result from his rejection of Medlow's offer, he must convince himself that his efforts are not in vain, that they will significantly benefit those who, like the boy, lack strong black male role models. Arguably, this need for social affirmation explains why Procter, an atheist, advises the boy to pray for him if he is taken away and beaten by the white police for not following the "rules." "I don't believe in God," Procter confesses to the boy, "But I want you to believe. I want you to believe He can hear you. That's the only way I'll be able to take those beatings—with you praying" (153). Read metaphorically, the boy's prayers represent the kind of cultural support that is necessary to promote social change and allow black men to acquire "manhood."

Although "Three Men" provides a provocative and insightful strategy for black male resistance, it stops short of addressing the complexities that adhere to putting such a strategy into practice. Taking up the problem of social implementation, *Always Outnumbered* highlights the difficulties that Socrates encounters when, on two separate occasions, he puts his notions of survival and liberation to the test. In the first (outlined briefly in the opening of this chapter), Socrates becomes the de facto leader of a local gathering of men who must decide how to rid their community of a junkie, Petis, who killed one of their own for drug money. In the second, Socrates has to decide whether to alert the police to a black arsonist who has unintentionally killed two innocent black indigents in one of his fires. Both situations bring Socrates's moral and cultural politics to the fore, highlighting the type of realistic challenges faced by those trying to "make a difference" in the black community.

In regard to the first dilemma, Socrates is compelled to reject both offers that Right and Markham present him—to either kill Petis or turn him over to the police—because at this stage in his intellectual and cultural development he is aware of how each contributes to implosive victimization. Having killed a black man in jail for physically and sexually molesting his much weaker cell mate, Socrates recognizes that killing, however valid and justifiable, undermines the cultural and moral fiber of the black community and the killer. He expresses this sentiment to Right, saying that "bein' right won't wash the blood from your hands" (30). The play on "right" here calls attention to the ethical and moral problem of using murder as a cultural policing strategy. The issue, then, is not whether Petis *deserves* to be killed, but what gives them the right to kill him.

Socrates also views involving the police in this instance as being complicit in oppression. Invoking images of slavery, he tells Markham that turning a black man in to the police, regardless of his crime, is ultimately a "hurt to all of us." "Goin' to the cops ovah a brother," he continues, "is like askin' for chains" (32). The slavery imagery is relevant here because it calls attention to the history of white male brutality against black men. Socrates links white policemen with slave overseers to underscore how police brutality is simply another mode of the violence that has historically been used to terrorize and control black men. Given this line of reasoning, to report Petis to the police is to sanction police brutality against all black men.

Despite Socrates's keen insights regarding murder and the police, his compromise—to force Petis out of the community—ultimately fails. Employing the use of violence to rid themselves of Petis, Socrates and his group reproduce the destructive cycle of black-on-black male violence that has so crippled the black community. Socrates is clearly aware of this pitfall, admonishing a member of the group for suggesting that the men become a more permanent policing force in the community. "We ain't some kinda gangbangers," Socrates says, "We cain't live like that" (36). By linking their organized attempt to combat crime in their community to gangbanging, he calls attention to the social and cultural problems resulting from the use of violence as a mechanism of resistance. In particular, he conveys that using violence as a cultural policing strategy exacerbates rather than improves social conditions in the community because it privileges violent interaction over more productive and healthy methods of conflict resolution.

Seeking to find an alternative to violence as a policing strategy, Socrates revises his earlier perspective on police involvement in black affairs. When he learns the identity of a black arsonist who has allegedly killed two black indigents in one of the many fires he has set, he solicits the aid of a black policeman. This is an especially difficult decision for Socrates, given his long history dealing with corrupt, abusive cops, black and white. The question then emerges: Why does Socrates pursue a black cop over a white one? Race matters for Socrates because even though it does not reveal anything substantive about one's character, it suggests something about the set of experiences that are likely to have shaped one's sense of reality. He is reticent to trust whites because they have few, if any, experiences that would allow them to understand the extent that race informs black life.

The politics of this racial dynamic are most dramatically displayed when Socrates exposes the racial biases of his young, good-hearted white coworker Bruce Tynan in a veiled conversation regarding the black arsonist and social justice. When Socrates asks Bruce what he would do if he knew of a man who had killed two people, Bruce responds confidently, "I'd go to the police." Pressing the issue, Socrates asks, "But what if . . . it wasn't on purpose?" The boy retorts, "Then they'd find him innocent in court" (173). More to himself than the boy, Socrates responds, "Naw. It was a mistake but he was doin' somethin' wrong. They'd still fry his ass" (173). Socrates's probing questions expose how Bruce's blind faith in the judicial system is bound up in his racial privilege as a white male. His most salient privilege is that he is not forced on a daily basis to think about race and its effect on his life. To this end, Bruce illustrates the main point of Peggy Macintosh's classic essay "White privilege: Unpacking the Invisible Knapsack." Macintosh discloses "a pattern running through the matrix of white privilege, a pattern of assumptions that were passed on to me as a white person. There was one main piece of cultural turf; it was my own turf, and I was among those who could control the turf. My skin color was an asset for any move I was educated to want to make. I could think of myself as belonging in major ways and of making social systems work for me. I could freely disparage, fear, neglect, or be oblivious to anything outside of the dominant cultural forms. Being of the main culture, I could also criticize it freely" (81).

Little wonder that Bruce is perplexed when Socrates summarily rejects his rationale. He has never been forced to contend seriously with the social realities of nonwhites and is oblivious to how racism informs the lives and perspectives of blacks. Fundamentally, Bruce can afford to have faith in social systems because he feels that those institutions are designed with his best interest in mind. Given the racial blind spots that white privilege engenders, it is certainly understandable that Socrates does not consider relaying his information about the black arsonist to Bruce or a white cop.

At bottom, Socrates's implicitly essentialist perspective on blackness is tactically necessary, given the violent relationship between cops and black men in poor urban communities. For

Socrates and other poor black men, understanding the racial politics of the police is quite literally a matter of life and death. However, in that some black cops advance the aims of white privilege (as illustrated in *Always Outnumbered*), race is certainly not a fail-safe signifier of cultural consciousness. Clearly aware of this fact, Socrates asks Folger, a retired police dispatcher, to put him in contact with a black cop who "knows he's black." For Socrates, to be "black" means to have a genuine commitment to and respect for black people. In regard to black cops specifically, it means treating alleged black male offenders humanely, providing them with due process rather than brutalizing them like animals and assuming their guilt.

Ironically, even as Socrates is able to find such a cop in Shreve, the man Folger refers him to, Socrates's decision to involve the police ultimately fails; the arsonist commits suicide when the police enter his yard. The thematic significance of the arsonist's death is illuminated during Socrates's conversation with his friend Stony shortly after the death. Lamenting his decision to involve the police, Socrates reflects, "I thought that I could make a difference. You know if I said I wouldn't cooperate [with the police] unless they promised to play fair?" (180). Stony responds, "They played fair, Socco . . . How could they help it if the man sees 'em comin' an' shoots hisself? You can't blame the cops for everything" (180). Though his comments are well intended, Stony trivializes the arsonist's death by absolving the police of responsibility. In short, he ignores the larger sociohistorical dynamics such as police brutality, racial profiling, and judicial injustice that informed the arsonist's response to the police. In doing so, Stony inadvertently blames the victim for his own victimization. Little wonder, then, that Socrates is offended almost to the point of violence by Stony's comments. He clearly recognizes the far-reaching social and cultural implications of Stony's apathy.

Underscoring the problematics of this apathy, Socrates sets fire to a hundred-dollar bill after Stony queries him about whether he received any reward money for identifying the black arsonist. After grabbing the bill from Socrates and putting the fire out, Stony asks emphatically, "What's wrong wit' you? This here's a hundred dollars" (181). Socrates responds coldly, "And it's yours, Stony. That's your share for helpin' t' kill Ponzelle" (181). Burning the hundred-dollar bill demonstrates that the "real" tragedy in this instance is that Stony is more concerned about the money than with the loss of another black life. That Socrates offers the money to Stony as compensation for his participation in the arsonist's death is telling. In effect, Socrates's sardonic offering casts light on another aspect of implosive victimization—namely, how blacks are encouraged, literarily and symbolically, to "sell" each other out.

Focused on the question of how to reverse the implosive victimization outlined in *Always Outnumbered,* Mosley's *Walkin' the Dog* stresses the need for blacks generally and black men specifically to create new resistance paradigms. At issue here are the conventional notions of black male resistance, which are premised on two deeply problematic notions that obscure the ways that unexamined black anger contributes to implosive victimization. The first is that the experience of oppression necessarily endows blacks with acute insight into the ideological and social mechanisms of their victimization. The second is that any and all types of retaliation to white oppression are justified by the extent of abuse that black men have incurred at the hands of whites. The inherent fallacies of both notions become evident during Socrates's conversation with Lavant Hall, a self-proclaimed revolutionary who steals an expensive dog from a rich white woman in the name of social justice. When Socrates asks Lavant to explain his act, Lavant responds, "It's a war out here, brother . . . They wanna make us into slaves with the dollar. They wanna make us into slaves next to the TV. They even wanna make you a slave to taxes, my brother. You pay 'em yo' money an' they use it to buy your chains" (153). Unmoved by Lavant's political rhetoric, Socrates responds, "I done heard all that shit in the lockup. All day long you hear men talk about bein' political prisoners an' all that shit. What I wanna know is what's all that got to do with you stealin' that woman's dog?" (153). Undeterred by Socrates's probing question, Lavant responds gleefully, "I didn't steal 'im I freed 'im . . . I'm a freedom fighter. That's my job twenty-four hours a day, seven days a week. While you sleepin' I'm out fightin' for freedom. While you makin' chains I'm putting acid in the locks" (155).

Portraying himself as a political rebel and Socrates as an unwitting slave to white capitalism, Lavant excuses his theft as an act of civil disobedience, a challenge to the white status quo. Ironically and humorously, he characterizes the dog as a slave to the rich woman. For Lavant, to take the dog from the rich woman is to strike out against white bondage. Closer scrutiny, however, reveals that Lavant is deeply invested in the white status quo. Fundamentally, he steals the dog because he is envious of the white woman's wealth, as he admits: "I saw this woman wearing a fur coat that was probably chinchilla. I say that 'cause the fur was like feathers, like Johnny [his stolen dog] look . . . But you know that white woman made me mad. There she had that cute dog and she was wearin' ten or twelve other animals on 'er back that looked just like him [the dog], at least their hair did" (152). While Lavant frames his resentment toward the white woman in a language that suggests protest against cruelty to animals, the real source of his anger is jealousy. He is "mad" because as a black man in a racist society he has limited access to the kind of wealth that the white woman can so casually flaunt. Stealing the expensive dog then becomes a way of recovering some of the material wealth that he feels blacks are owed for past suffering. Ironically, since she can probably buy many more dogs, he does not recover anything. What he does is cause her momentary pain that makes him feel powerful. Aware that Lavant's misplaced ideas of resistance politics obscure the ethical problems of his theft and his investment in the white status quo, Socrates states, "I still don't see why you stole that dog" (154). Then, in mocking the situation, he turns to his own dog, Killer, and remarks sardonically, "Let's get you home before somebody wants to make you free" (154).

The most probing critiques of how unexamined black anger contributes to implosive victimization occur in Socrates's animated conversations with his weekly black discussion group. Focusing on the link between implosive victimization and the historical sources of black anger, Mosley demonstrates how cultural assumptions regarding black "innocence" in oppression discourage blacks from addressing their roles in their own subjugation. Addressing these cultural assumptions is a necessary corrective to the anesthetizing effect of white hate and blame on black liberation efforts. Viewing themselves as blameless victims because of past and present suffering, blacks feel that the bulk of responsibility for ending white oppression lies with the oppressors. Such a view is dangerous not only because it gives blacks a false sense of moral and social innocence, but because it inadvertently reinforces the notion that whites have the power to dictate black behavior. Ultimately, by displacing social responsibility on to whites, blacks relinquish their social agency.

The problematic elements of this viewpoint underscore the importance of a black male feminist perspective. Illuminating how intraracial gender dynamics inform such claims to innocence inter- and intraracially, a black male feminist perspective exposes the contradictory assumptions that underlie victimization discourses. Mosley illustrates these assumptions in an early conversation that Socrates has with his discussion group. Cynthia and Veronica—the only two female members in the group—initiate this discussion when they take one of the men to task for claiming that a lack of male leadership is to blame for the disintegration of the black community. Cynthia responds forcefully that "a man wanna rattle his sword and shake his fist. A man wanna lead and the rest wanna follow. But when that man is cut down, we're lost. The head is gone, the man is gone and all the plans is gone too. A man, no matter how good he is, makes a mess" (142). Agreeing with Cynthia, Veronica chimes in, "I don't want no man out there yellin' and fightin' when he could be [at] home wit' me . . . It breaks my heart when they [whites] kill our men . . . or when they [black men] kill each other" (142).

Responding specifically to Veronica's reference to black-on-black homicide, Socrates asks, "But what else can we do?" (142). He continues, "It's like nobody listens . . . It's like you always alone. Most of the time it's like you got to yell or hit or somethin' 'cause nobody's listenin'. You got to do somethin'. You got to let somebody know. Other people don't have that problem. One of 'em look to the other one and they both nod and they know" (142). When asked by one of the men to clarify his statements, Socrates adds, "I don't know [what I'm talking about] . . . But it's somethin'. Cynthia's right. Other people don't have a leader you could point to and they seem okay. You got your Chinese in Chinatown and your Koreans with their language all over billboards and stores up on Olympic. And the Jews all over the country help each other without sayin' they need another Moses to set 'em free" (142).

At first glance, Socrates appears to contradict himself. Even as he concedes Cynthia's point (that black propensity for violence and control hampers black resistance efforts), he implies that violence is the only viable means by which black men can express their social alienation. Closer scrutiny, however, reveals that Socrates's ambivalence about black male violence is linked to the problematic idea of black resistance that he has internalized—in particular, the notion that blacks comprehend the complexity of their oppression and how to end it. Socrates's ambivalence toward black violence shows that he is grappling with notions of racial solidarity and social innocence that undergird street-level nationalism for black men. Implicitly, he realizes that a simple assumption of racial solidarity and social innocence does not account for, or adequately explain, the social isolation many black men experience, isolation that prompts them to take out their social frustrations on each other. The Chinese, Koreans, and Jews do not experience the need to "be heard" or socially validated at the level of blacks because, Socrates believes, these ethnic groups have a more stable cultural base from which to negotiate the racist practices of white America. Lacking an equivalent base, black men experience a kind of cultural identity crisis.

By invoking the cultural stability of other minority groups, Socrates expresses a key aspect of Mosley's cultural critique: the idea that what blacks have in common is suffering, rather than a distinct cultural ethos. This distinction is important because it explains why it is so difficult for black men to make sense of their oppression. Forced, because of social and cultural circumstances, to view themselves through the lens of their oppressors, black men have to contend with the perceptions of their reality that whites impose upon them, perceptions that ostensibly deny them their humanity. As James Baldwin insightfully observes in "Many Thousands Gone," when blacks internalize the white assumption that "to be truly human and acceptable" they must become in character like their white oppressors, blacks "can only acquiesce in the obliteration of . . . [their] own personality, surrendering to those forces which reduce the person to anonymity" (45).

In "Harlem Is Nowhere" Ralph Ellison further explores the social and psychological implications of cultural fragmentation for black men. Ellison argues that when black men are barred from full participation in the main institutional life of society, "[t]hey lose one of the bulwarks which men place between themselves and the constant threat of chaos. For whatever the assigned function of social institutions, their psychological function is to protect the citizen against the irrational, incalculable forces that hover about the edges of human life like cosmic destruction lurking within an atomic stockpile" (299). Ellison further notes that because black men have to contend with both the tensions that arise from their "own swift history" and those "conflicts created in modern man by a revolutionary world," they cannot fully participate "in the therapy which the white American achieves through patriotic ceremonies and by identifying [themselves] with American wealth and power. Instead, [black men are] thrown back upon their own 'slum-shocked' institutions" (300). They resort to violence (and other kinds of self-destructive behavior), Ellison implies, because they have no institutional support to validate their experiences of suffering and oppression.

Even as Socrates and Mosley highlight the problems of cultural fragmentation, they are clearly more concerned with how this fragmentation informs black-on-black homicide than with charting white participation in this process. This concern is brought into focus by Socrates's response to Chip Lowe, another member of the group, who asks him what his earlier comments about the lack of black cultural stability "mean" for blacks. Socrates states plainly, "It means that I'm tired, man . . . We dyin' out here" (142). When Veronica presses Socrates to clarify his statement, he says, "It's like there's somethin' missin'. Somethin' I ain't got in my head. I know what's wrong but I don't know what's right. You know what I mean?" (143). Focusing attention on how black men have become their own worst enemies, Socrates illuminates the disjuncture between the theory and practice of black resistance. Implicitly, he recognizes that if black men truly understood the complexities of their oppression, they would not be killing each other at such alarming rates.

Mosley investigates this disjuncture further when Nelson, the owner of the funeral parlor, challenges Socrates's implicit claims about black political consciousness. Nelson asserts confidently, "We [blacks] all know what's right, Socrates" (142). Socrates retorts dismissively, "All of us?" He then adds, "Then why do we have it so bad out here? Why don't we all get out in the street an' clean up what we got and then get together to take back what's been stolen?" (142). Before Nelson can complete his rejoinder (which continues in the same oppositional racial vein), Socrates interjects, "I know what it is [that] stop[s] me" from doing something. "It's cause I'd be alone out there. I'd be crazy because I'm the only one and how can one man matter? It's like a butterfly in a hurricane"(143). Socrates's comments regarding black social resignation are insightful. Casting light on how blacks have failed to use even the limited social agency they do possess to alter society, he addresses the limitations—political, social, and psychological— of resistance strategies premised on blame. For Socrates such strategies discourage rather than encourage social action because they

are structured on the idea that if whites relinquish their oppression of blacks, then most of the social problems plaguing the black community would inevitably dissipate. Placing the responsibility to change their oppressive behavior on whites, this perspective inadvertently exonerates the oppressed of any responsibility to promote social change.

Socrates's striking butterfly-in-the-hurricane analogy illuminates Mosley's resistance strategy, which is premised on the idea that individual acts of struggle produce huge social and cultural results. Invoking a key image from the scientific field of chaos theory, this analogy conveys a far different perspective on individual social agency than is Socrates's original intent. Specifically, it invokes what Edward Lorenz called the butterfly effect—the theory that minute changes in local conditions can have a substantial impact on global weather patterns. According to this theory, the chain of events set off by the flapping of a butterfly's wings in, say, Great Britain could feasibly determine whether a hurricane would strike Jamaica or a blizzard would occur in Chicago. The pervasiveness of such small changes in the atmosphere makes it impossible to predict in advance which small events will have huge consequences. Read paradoxically, then, Socrates's analogy attests to the potential significance of individual struggle against formidable forces. Though he invokes the analogy to explain why he does not challenge the status quo, his one-man protest against the "hurricane" of white supremacy in the Los Angeles Police Department is a stunning illustration of the butterfly effect. Though seemingly up against insurmountable odds, his protest unexpectedly generates enough social unrest to shut down the city of Los Angeles for nearly a week and attract international attention.

Socrates's awareness of his individual agency is further heightened when he gets a substantial job promotion and moves to a more upscale and safer neighborhood. That Mosley has Socrates's eventual comprehension of his individual and cultural agency coincide with his elevation to the middle class is certainly significant. Clearly, Mosley wants to underscore the critical role that econom-

ics play in the process of Socrates's political development. Mosley is not, however, positing a simple link between middle-class values and black empowerment. Rather he points up how difficult it is for poor urban blacks to devote time and energy to critiquing their resistance politics in the midst of such extreme poverty, violence, and crime. To this end, Socrates's new environment is essential to his political development because it offers him a break from the daily physical and psychological pressures of ghetto life. This physical and psychological reprieve allows him the necessary space and time to contemplate his racial oppression and begin the process of working through issues of anger and violence. In this new environment, the narrator reports, Socrates "could believe that he was the master" (224).

Socrates's new insights are highlighted during a political discussion he facilitates in his new home. Revisiting the issue of white blame and black-on-black homicide, Socrates opens the meeting with a probing and provocative question: "What I wanna know is if you think that black people have a right to be mad at white folks or are we all just fulla shit an' don't have no excuse for misery down here an' everywhere else" (219). This question is important in that it draws attention to the problematics of the victim/victimizer binary conventionally used to frame black/white power relations and justify anger and resentment directed against whites. Premised on the static notion that blacks are helpless (and thereby blameless) victims of white oppression, this binary generates the kind of cultural despondency that initially makes Socrates feel socially powerless. His provocative question illustrates that he has come to terms, at least partly, with the agency that he and blacks possess to alter their social circumstances. By suggesting that blacks may not be blameless and may actually function as (self) victimizers, Socrates raises critical questions about the nature and complexity of black suffering. Such as: what is the connection between suffering and victimhood? Does suffering necessarily render the victimized innocent and blameless? To what extent are whites responsible for black social problems? To what extent are black social problems self-created?

Mosley engages these complex issues of victimhood in the heated and gendered debate that follows Socrates's question. Emphasizing the disparate gender perspectives on white blame, Mosley illustrates how intraracial gender politics complicate perspectives on black complicity and victimization. The most revealing argument emerges between Leon Spellman and Cynthia Lott—two of the most vocal members of the group—over which gender suffers the most. The argument is ignited when Cynthia presses Leon to explain why he supports Nelson's statement (in response to Socrates's initial question) that blacks already "know what's been done to us that's wrong . . . [and] what we got to do to make our lives better." Cynthia asks sardonically, "What is it you know?"—to which Leon responds confidently, "I know I'm a black man in a white world that had me as a slave; that keeps me from my history and my birthright" (221). Challenging Leon's problematic notion of black (male) suffering, Cynthia responds, "First off you ain't a man you're a boy. You wasn't never a slave. And as far as any birthright you live wit' your momma and play at like you tryin' to go to school. As far as I see it you ain't got nuthin' to complain about at all. I mean if you cain't make somethin' outta yourself with all that you got then all they could blame is you" (222).

Cynthia calls Leon's claim to victimhood into question on the basis of what she perceives to be his failed manhood. From her vantage point, Leon has no "right" to blame whites for his debilitating circumstances because he has taken no personal initiative to alter his situation. That Leon still lives at homes with his mother is evidence enough for Cynthia that he has shirked his manly responsibilities. The "real" victims, Cynthia implies, are Leon's mother and black women like her who have had to shoulder the emotional, social, and economic burden of irresponsible black men. Cynthia makes these feelings explicit when Socrates tries to mediate by interjecting, "But I didn't ask if he [Leon] could blame somebody, Cyn . . . I asked if we got the right to be mad. All us is mad. Almost every black man, woman or child you meet is mad . . . Even if you blame Leon for his problems you still sayin' that there's something wrong. Ain't you?" To this she responds forcefully, "Only thing wrong is that these here men you got today ain't worth shit . . . Black men puffin' up an' blamin' anybody they can. He say 'I cain't get a job 'cause'a the white man,' or, 'I can't stay home 'cause Mr. Charlie on my butt.' But the woman is home. The woman got a job and a child and a pain in her heart that don't stop. I don't know why I wanna be mad at no white man when I got a black man willin' to burn me down to the ground and then stomp on my ashes" (222).

Refocusing the debate onto male-female issues, Cynthia takes Socrates and black men to task for their patriarchal rendering of black suffering as that of black men only. She draws attention to ways that black men have used white oppression to justify socioeconomic irresponsibility, on the one hand, and their abuse of black women on the other. Significantly, Cynthia spotlights the problem of associating suffering with blamelessness, echoing Morrison's argument in *Paradise* that white oppression does not exempt black men from being victimizers.

Cynthia's perspective on black male victimization is not without its problems, however. Like Velma in *The Salt Eaters*, she characterizes black women as the ultimate victims, the only group with a legitimate right to be angry and to cast blame. In doing so she falls prey to the kind of gendered scapegoating and posturing that corrupts the resistance politics of Velma and the sisters of the yam. Claiming ultimate victimization as a black woman, Cynthia reproduces a problematic notion of victimhood similar to what she rejects in regard to black men.

Veronica highlights the problems of Cynthia's perspective when she acknowledges the failings of black women: "you know ain't no man start out perfect. No woman neither. I know a lotta black women out here mess up just as quick as a man. Quicker sometimes" (223). Acknowledging that black women "mess up" too, Veronica indicates the inherent problems of Cynthia's sweeping indictment of black men. In effect, Veronica shows that by privileging black women's suffering over men's, Cynthia slips into a version of the "blame game" that she ostensibly repudiates.

The story of a slave rebellion that Socrates relays to his group in the midst of their bickering over "who suffers the most" provides insights into how blaming and scapegoating whites (and each other) undermines black resistance strategies. Based on a group of twenty-two Louisiana slaves who kill their slave masters and become a formidable band of rebels (the rascals in the cane), the story reveals how even those who have suffered unimaginable persecution and hardship can be corrupted by revenge, hate, and guilt. Even as the rascals in the cane were able (because of their superior guerrilla tactics) to force the white plantation owners to fear and respect them, their rebellion was sullied because, in killing their slave masters, they violated their own sacred beliefs about murder. Socrates reports that the rascals in the cane were afraid that "if they ever left the swamplands and the cane [to which they escaped] they would be hunted down and killed for their sins. Because they knew that killin' was wrong. They knew they had murdered old Drummond and Langley Whitehall, the plantation owner, and his family and men. So they stayed in the wild and went kinda crazy" (227).

Rather than motivating them to find an alternative to murder, their guilt and shame become the driving forces behind their continued struggle, during which they murder other blacks who refuse to join their ranks. In effect, the rascals in the cane succumb to similar social and cultural problems that plague the men of Ruby in Morrison's *Paradise*. Like the Ruby men, the rascals in the cane are unwilling to come to terms with their own social and ethical failings. Rather, they scapegoat and terrorize other blacks to displace and hide their feelings of guilt and shame. Socrates notes that if rascals "came up on a slave . . . [who] was too scared to go with 'em then they would say that that slave was their enemy and . . . kill him" (227). That the rascals begin to murder other runaway blacks is telling. Once they compromise their own moral and ethical beliefs regarding murder, the rebels become increasingly like their oppressors, using their power to intimidate others into conforming to their social standards and political values. Their suffering under slavery had filled them with homicidal rage rather than providing them with insight into their oppression. Instead of exhibiting compassion for the runaway slaves who choose not to join them, the rebels in the cane show only murderous contempt.

Although Socrates does not fully comprehend the link between his story and the original question concerning black agency and white blame (as his befuddled responses to the questions generated by his narrative reveal), his reflections after the meeting foreshadow his eventual political and cultural revelation. Socrates "realized that it wasn't just white people that made him mad. He would be upset even if there weren't any white people" (231). He then engages in an imaginary conversation with his deceased aunt Bellandra, who first told him the story about the rascals in the cane. Reflecting on the slave narrative, he asks, "How come they didn't go down into Mexico?" His aunt responds, "Because the road wasn't paved" (231). Recalling Velma's communications with the elders in *The Salt Eaters,* Socrates's nighttime reflections and his imaginary conversation with his dead aunt reveal the problems of conventional notions of resistance premised on white blame and hatred. Focused as they are on white responsibility in black oppression, these notions are encouragement to blacks to ignore other intraracial social issues that are not necessarily linked to white oppression. As such, they limit the ways that blacks can conceptualize the myriad complexities of their lives. White oppression becomes a master narrative for understanding other social issues, obscuring how internal cultural factors contribute to the disintegration of the black community. Socrates's revelation regarding the complexity of his anger is important, then, because it reveals how black preoccupation with white hatred/blame forestalls deeper investigations into intraracial matters.

The imaginary conversation, a mode of communication with the ancestral wisdom of the black community, situates the issue of white blame and hatred within a larger historical context. In doing so, it reveals how ancestral suffering informs the anger that many blacks harbor against whites and each other. For

Socrates to resolve his issues of hatred toward whites (and black-on-black violence), he must come to grips with how similar feelings have corrupted the resistance efforts of his slave ancestors. Aunt Bellandra's response to young Socrates's inquiry speaks to this dynamic. Her reference to the unpaved road can be read as the failure of the rascals in the cane to consider alternatives to violent resistance. Their demise, then, is due in part to their inability to move beyond the impasse of a resistance paradigm premised on hatred, guilt, and revenge. Failing to create an alternative to fighting, they not only replicate the destructive practices of their oppressors, they terrorize and murder other innocent blacks. The link between Socrates's slave past and his current dilemmas with anger and black-on-black violence becomes clear. To avoid repeating the destructive pattern, he must learn from his ancestors' mistakes and create new, more constructive modes of resistance.

The final scene of the *Walkin' the Dog* focuses on the process of creating this alternative resistance strategy. His hatred toward whites still unresolved, Socrates finds himself stalking Matthew G. Cardwell, a rogue white cop responsible for brutalizing a young man, raping a black woman, and murdering a fourteen-year-old boy. The link between the past and present is illuminated when the narrator reports that Socrates began to stalk Cardwell "with no intention except to nurse a feeling of hatred that was so familiar [that] he sometimes wondered if the hate was older than him" (239). The historical and cultural complexity of Socrates's hatred is again revealed when he conjures up his deceased aunt's reflections on slavery and black men. She says, "The chains on a black man . . . go down through the centuries. They once made us slaves to the plantation but now they make us slaves to the slaves we was . . . A good word and a gentle touch is like a cloud that passes on a nice day . . . But pain, real pain last forever. It hurt your son and his son and his. The slave is still cryin' even though his chains ain't nuthin but rust, even though he's long gone and forgotten" (239).

Consumed by hatred, Socrates misreads his aunt's rumination on black suffering as a call to arms. He surmises that killing Cardwell will fulfill some kind of cultural destiny. As Socrates anxiously waits in ambush for Cardwell, the narrator reports, "The murder in the air came through his lungs and from there to his blood. Socrates, who knew that he had been prepared for centuries, was finally ready to answer a destiny older than the oldest man in the world" (240). Clearly, Socrates seeks revenge not only for the crimes that Cardwell has committed against blacks in his community, but for those that whites have historically committed against blacks. At this point, he fails to realize that the "hurt" to which his aunt speaks is partially due to the destructive manner in which black men have responded to white oppression.

The epiphany that compels Socrates to spare Cardwell's life marks his cultural and ideological breakthrough. Explaining this epiphany to Darryl the day after he nearly kills Cardwell, Socrates says, "It was the air, no, no, no, the breath of air . . . I mean it was so good. I mean good, man. You know I almost called out loud. I saw Cardwell walkin' my way an' my hands was tight on them guns. You know he was a dead man an' didn't know it. I pulled them pistols outta my pockets. I was thinking about him dyin' but at the same time I was wonderin' what was goin' on in my mind. You know what I mean, Darryl? How you could think about somethin' an' still be thinkin' bout somethin' else?" (241)

Though Socrates experiences his epiphany as a sudden appreciation of life, his insights come from the connections that he is finally able to make between his ancestral past and present. The dream that he has the night after his epiphany elucidates these connections. Described appropriately as a "variation on an old theme" (242), this dream recalls an earlier one that Socrates has in *Always Outnumbered*. In the first dream, he is forced by a giant black man to dig up the graves of thousands of blacks who "had died from grief" (*Always Outnumbered*, 94). Emphasizing the need for Socrates to examine the link between his own grief and that of his ancestors, this dream anticipates his cultural and ideological breakthrough. In the second dream, the giant black man reappears to confirm Socrates's new insights and to challenge him to make use of them. He says, "I only wanna know what you gonna do now. You done the first job. You done dug up all the dead an' set 'em free. Now what you gonna do with all that power?" (242). The "first job" was clearly to examine his slave legacy in order to learn about the complex source of his ancestors' suffering: that which was directly caused by white oppression, and that which was self-induced. Having successfully completed that job, Socrates is able to reconcile his hatred of whites because he has a more complete understanding of the problems of black anger. This knowledge is "power" because it allows him, intellectually and emotionally, to move beyond the cultural barriers of white hatred and blame, barriers that inadvertently reify implosive victimization and black social resignation.

Socrates does not fully comprehend the significance of his cultural insights, however, until after he launches a one-man protest against Cardwell. His initial objective is simply to stand up against his oppressors without resorting to violence. Having become aware of the larger historical and cultural implications of his own actions, he knows that "killing, even killing someone like Cardwell, was a mark on your soul. And not only on you but on all the black men and women who were alive, and those who were to come after, and those who were to come after that too" (254). Even though the success of Socrates's gesture far exceeds his expectations, he remains ambivalent about the final outcome of his protest. While his bloodless protest forces the city to suspend Cardwell, it does not have much impact on how blacks regard their individual and collective social agency; when Cardwell is suspended they return to their social routines. Given this response from the black community, Socrates views his protest as having ultimately failed.

Shortly after his release from prison Socrates tries to explain this failure to Nelson, who feels that Socrates is wasting a valuable political opportunity by refusing to speak to the press. Nelson opines, "You got power now. You got the ear of the press. You could make a difference out here" (256). Socrates replies incredulously, "I know what you sayin', Nelson . . . But it ain't nuthin' I could say that they [whites] don't already know. Them reporters know all about Cardwell an' cops like him. They know all about men who been in prison. They already know. It's us [blacks] that don't know" (256–57). Socrates rejects Nelson's plea partly because he knows that the mainstream media is vested in promoting the ideas and views of the dominant culture, and partly because he rejects conventional resistance strategies geared to reform racist white attitudes.

To appeal to white sympathies is fruitless, Socrates implies, because whites have no social or economic impetus to change their behavior toward blacks. For him the central problem lies with the black community. Having incurred centuries of physical and psychological abuse, blacks have lost sight of the full spectrum of their social and political agency. As a result, they tolerate abuses that are well within their power to eliminate. Preoccupied as he is with black suffering and white blame, Nelson is unable to process Socrates's argument. Specifically, Nelson has difficulty conceptualizing blacks as more than victims of white oppression and misreads Socrates's insights on black empowerment as a denial of black suffering. Perplexed, he retorts, "Every black man, woman and child knows what it's like to be poor and mistreated and held back. Even me. You know they didn't wanna know about me at the funeral director's society. I had to make all kindsa stink just to belong . . . What do you mean that we're the ones who don't know?" Socrates responds, "We had the whole city scared, Nelson. But nuthin' changed. No one said, 'Hey, lets get together an' vote or strike or just get together and say somethin' true.' Me complainin' to some newspaper is like me tellin' the warden that I don't like his jail" (257). Clearly, Socrates is aware of the suffering that blacks have incurred at the hands of whites. However, he is also aware of how blacks have preoccupied themselves with this suffering to the point of enabling white oppression. This preoccupation with suffering, then, explains why the black community is so easily pacified by Cardwell's suspension even as they are cognizant that he is but one of many racist and abusive policemen. Having for so long underestimated the extent of their social power, they have lowered their expectations for social justice. Given these low expectations, they interpret a minor social gain (like getting a racist cop suspended from his job) as a major political victory. Acutely attuned to this cultural dynamic, Socrates knows that unless blacks begin to demand more of themselves and whites, they will continue to be treated as second-class citizens.

The black male feminist politics that underlie *Always Outnumbered* and *Walkin' the Dog* illuminate the complex and myriad ways that unexamined historical black anger frustrates black resistance efforts, fomenting gender discord and black-on-black male violence. Even though there have been novels that have engaged all these cultural issues in some form, few have probed as deeply into the historical source and complexity of the gendered black anger that informs them. The intraracial taboos that have kept these important issues from receiving serious attention are certainly not baseless. Whites continue to use one-sided hegemonic cultural reasoning to stereotype blacks as irresponsible, immoral, violent, and anti-intellectual. Speaking to this dynamic for black men, Nelson rightly concludes that "if one black man commits a crime then we are all seen as criminals. All of us share that legacy" (*Walkin' the Dog* 223). Refusing to accept the cultural logic that shapes the impasse, Mosley challenges blacks to move beyond the ideological barriers created by white hegemonic thinking. Implicitly, he understands that while blacks cannot control how whites (mis)treat them, socially and economically, they can control how they respond to this (mis)treatment. Reclaiming this control (despite the potential political repercussions of acknowledging complicity) is a necessary step toward altering black racial realities in America. The social cost of this reclamation, as Socrates demonstrates, may be extremely high. However, the crucial question that emerges is: Can blacks afford not to pay it? To invoke Baby Suggs's advice to Denver in Morrison's *Beloved*, we must reconcile ourselves to the harsh reality of our struggle, "Know it, and [then] go on out the yard" (244).

CONCLUSION

IN W. E. B. DU BOIS'S lesser-known essay "My Evolving Program for Negro Freedom," he reveals the ways that discrimination and white exploitation altered his perspective on racial uplift and whites. Convinced that misinformation was the chief catalyst of racial inequality, Du Bois set out early in his career to use science to disprove white notions of black inferiority. Naively, he believed that whites would be compelled to end racial discrimination if they were presented with hard evidence to dispel racial myths. However, many years of testing this hypothesis showed him that racism was not so much the product of misinformation as it was the result of social convention. He writes: "[T]he majority of men do not usually act in accord with reason, but follow social pressures, inherited customs and long-established, often sub-conscious, patterns of action. Consequently, race prejudice in America will linger long and may even increase." To this end, he continues, "[I]t is the duty of the black race to maintain its cultural advance, not for itself alone, but for the emancipation of mankind, the realization of democracy and the progress of civilization" (70).

Highlighting Du Bois's insights regarding race and racism is useful here because it helps to bring intraracial gender dilemmas into focus. More specifically, Du Bois underscores the difficulty of challenging dominant cultural ideologies and dismantling oppressive regimes. Considered within a racial-gendered context, his insights explain why extirpating black patriarchal thinking will require far more than attesting to the existence of black female oppression. The veracity of this claim is made most evident by how little the social circumstances of black women have changed in and beyond the academic arena despite successful attempts by black female feminists to bring black women's issues into public consciousness.

Unfortunately, many black male scholars are partly to blame for impeding the institutional success of black female feminist methodology. Threatened by critiques that implicated black men in the oppression of black women, they either disparaged black feminist criticism as culturally divisive or ignored its existence altogether. Even as they lacked the political and economic power of their white male counterparts, they were still able to rely on gendered cultural taboos against black male criticism to silence many would-be detractors. While this resistance to black feminist criticism has lessened significantly over the past decade, there are many black male scholars who are still hostile toward black feminism.

To root out this hostility and other negative responses to black women's issues, black male feminists will need to be rigorous and uncompromising in their critique of black patriarchal thinking. This means that all aspects of black gender and cultural issues are subject to critique, especially the heavily policed modes of thought that support black women's self-sacrifice and cast black men as agentless victims of emasculation within and beyond the black community. This approach to the dilemma of black patriarchal thinking allows for deeper investigations into intraracial gender privilege and abuse. Moreover, it also ensures that the issue of black female agency is not lost in discussions of black female victimization.

The black male feminist project is most useful because it strives to establish viable notions of black manhood that are not premised on black female subjugation. This is an important endeavor, considering that most cultural-gender criticism focuses almost exclusively on identifying the problems of black male identity. Even as this focus is understandable given the real social need to validate black female victimization, it provides few opportunities to engage the process of reconceptualizing black manhood. Identifying the underlining problems of black male identity is necessary for a productive approach to the problem of intraracial gender inequities. However, it is not the only step. It is equally as important to establish alternative models for black manhood to offset conventional ones.

A lot of work is certainly left to do as it relates to black male feminism. Unfortunately, few black male scholars are willing to take up the issue of intraracial gender inequities, choosing rather to rehearse established victimizer/victimized arguments that feature black men as the ultimate targets of white racist regimes. This unwillingness to acknowledge black female subjugation reflects the extent to which many black men have internalized the mindsets of their oppressors. In *The Fire Next Time* James Baldwin addresses this phenomenon indirectly when he argues that in order to alter their circumstances in society blacks must accept that their cultural identities are inextricably linked to those of whites. He writes, "[I]n order to change a situation one has first to see it for what it is: in the present case, to accept the fact . . . that the Negro has been formed by this nation, for better or for worse, and does not belong to any other" (81). Accepting this cultural reality is essential, Baldwin argues, because it allows blacks to recognize the extent to which they are implicated in the maintenance of their own victimization.

I would add to Baldwin's insights that in order for black men to alter their situation in America they must first realize that their past, present, and future are inextricably bound up with black women. Until they come to terms with this reality, any attempt at resistance will be tarnished by complicity in the white status quo. To invoke Baldwin again, "One can give nothing whatever without giving oneself—that is to say, risking oneself. If one cannot risk oneself, then one is simply incapable of giving. And, after all, one can give freedom only by setting someone free" (86).

Works Cited

Awkward, Michael. "A Black Man's Place(s) in Black Feminist Criticism." In *Representing Black Men*. Ed. Marcellus Blount and George P. Cunningham. New York: Routledge, 1996. 3–26.

———. *Negotiating Difference: Race, Gender, and the Politics of Positionality*. Chicago: U of Chicago P, 1995.

———. *Inspiriting Influences: Tradition, Revision, and Afro-American Women's Novels*. New York: Columbia UP, 1989.

———. "You're Turning Me On": The Boxer, the Beauty Queen, and the Rituals of Gender." In *Black Men on Race, Gender, and Sexuality*. Ed. Devon W. Carbado. New York: New York UP, 1999. 128–46.

Baldwin, James. *Go Tell It on the Mountain*. New York: Dell, 1952.

———. "Freaks and the American Ideal of Manhood." In *Baldwin: Collected Essays*. New York: Literary Classics of the US, 1998. 814–29.

———. "Many Thousands Gone." In *Notes of a Native Son*. Boston: Beacon, 1955.

———. *The Fire Next Time*. New York: Vintage, 1962.

Bambara, Toni Cade. *The Black Woman: An Anthology*. New York: New American Library, 1970.

———. *The Salt Eaters*. New York: Random House, 1980.

———. "What It Is I Think I'm Doing Anyhow." In *The Writer on Her Work*. Ed. Janet Stemburg. New York: Norton, 1980. 153–68.

———. "Voices beyond the Veil: An Interview with Toni Cade Bambara and Sonia Sanchez." In *Wild Women in the Whirlwind: Afra-American Culture and the Contemporary Literary Renaissance*. Ed. Joanne M. Braxton and Andrée Nicola McLaughlin. New Brunswick, NJ: Rutgers UP, 1990. 342–62.

Baraka, Amiri. "The Myth of a 'Negro Literature.'" In *Home: Social Essays*. New York: Morrow, 1966. 105–15.

———. *Dutchman, and The Slave; Two Plays*. London: Faber and Faber, 1965.

———. *The Autobiography of Leroi Jones/Amiri Baraka*. Chicago: Lawrence Hill, 1997.

Bouson, Brooks J. *Quiet As It's Kept: Shame, Trauma, and Race in the Novels of Toni Morrison*. Albany: State U of New York P, 2000.

Butler-Evans, Elliott. *Race, Gender, and Desire: Narrative Strategies in the Fiction of Toni Cade Bambara, Toni Morrison, and Alice Walker*. Philadelphia: Temple UP, 1989.

Byerman, Keith. *Fingering the Jagged Grain: Tradition and Form in Recent Black Fiction*. Athens: U of Georgia P, 1985.

Carbado, W. Devon. "Black Male Racial Victimhood." *Callaloo* 21.2 (1998): 337–61.

———. "The Construction of O. J. Simpson as a Racial Victim." In *Black Men on Race, Gender, and Sexuality*. Ed. Devon W. Carbado. New York: New York UP, 1999. 159–93.

Carby, Hazel. *Reconstructing Womanhood: The Emergence of the Afro-American Woman Novelist*. Oxford: Oxford UP, 1987.

Chesnutt, Charles. *The Marrow of Tradition*. Ed. Eric J. Sundquist. New York: Penguin, 1993.

Cleaver, Eldridge. *Soul on Ice*. New York: Random House, 1992.

Combahee River Collective. "A Black Feminist Statement." In *All the Women Are White and All the Blacks Are Men, But Some of Us Are Brave*. Ed. Gloria T. Hull, Patricia Bell Scott, and Barbara Smith. New York: Feminist Press, 1982. 13–22.

Crouch, Stanley. "Aunt Medea: *Beloved* by Toni Morrison." *New Republic* 19 (Oct. 1987): 38–43.

Douglass, Frederick. *Narrative of the Life of Frederick Douglass, An American Slave*. (1845). New York: Anchor Books, 1963.

Du Bois, W. E. B. *The Souls of Black Folk*. New York: Dover, 1994.

———. "My Evolving Program for Negro Freedom." *What the Negro Wants*. Ed. Rayford W. Logan. Chapel Hill: U of North Carolina P, 1944. 31–70.

Early, Gerald. *Daughters: On Family and Fatherhood*. Reading, MA: Addison-Wesley, 1994.

Ellison, Ralph. *Invisible Man*. New York: Vintage, 1947.

———. "Harlem Is Nowhere." In *Shadow and Act*. New York: Random House, 1953.

———. "Change the Joke and Slip the Yoke." In *Shadow and Act*. New York: Random House, 1953.

Fabre, Michel, and Edward Margolies. *The Several Lives of Chester Himes*. Jackson: UP of Mississippi, 1997.

Foster, Frances Smith. *Witnessing Slavery: The Development of Ante-bellum Slave Narratives*. Madison: U of Wisconsin P, 1979.

Gaines, Ernest. *Bloodline*. New York: Norton, 1976.

Gayle, Addison, Jr. *The Way of the New World: The Black Novel in America*. Garden City, NY: Anchor P, 1975.

Gilmore, Glenda E. "Murder, Memory, and the Flight of the Incubus." In *Democracy Betrayed: The Wilmington Race Riot of 1898 and Its Legacy*. Ed. David S. Cecelski and Timothy B. Tyson. Chapel Hill: U of North Carolina P, 1998.

Harris, Trudier. *Black Women in the Fiction of James Baldwin*. Knoxville: U of Tennessee P, 1985.

———. *Exorcising Blackness: Historical and Literary Lynching and Burning Rituals*. Bloomington: Indiana UP, 1984.

Hill Collins, Patricia. *Black Feminist Thought: Knowledge, Consciousness, and the Politics of Empowerment*. New York: Routledge, 1990.

Himes, Chester. *If He Hollers Let Him Go*. New York: Thunder's Mouth, 1945.

———. *My Life of Absurdity*. New York: Thunder's Mouth, 1976.

Hogness, Peter. "Down to the Crossroads." *Village Literary Supplement* 5 (Sept. 1995): 4.

hooks, bell. *Sisters of the Yam: Black Women and Self-Recovery*. Boston: South End, 1993.

Hurston, Zora Neale. *Their Eyes Were Watching God*. New York: Harper and Row, 1937.

King, Deborah. "Multiple Jeopardy, Multiple Consciousness: The Context of a Black Feminist Ideology." *Signs: Journal of Women in Culture and Society* 14.1 (1988): 42–72.

Kubitschek, Missy Dehn. *Toni Morrison: A Critical Companion*. Westport: Greenwood, 1998.

Lashgari, Deirdre. "Introduction: To Speak the Unspeakable: Implications of Gender, 'Race,' Class, and Culture." In *Violence, Silence, and Anger: Women's Writing as Transgression*. Ed. Deirdre Lashgari. U of Virginia P, 1995. 1–23.

Loomba, Ania. *Colonialism/Postcolonialism*. London: Routledge, 1998.

Macintosh, Peggy. "White Privilege: Unpacking the Invisible Knapsack." In *Beyond Heroes and Holidays: A Practical Guide to K–12 Anti-racist, Multicultural Education and Staff Development*. Ed. Enid Lee, Deborah Menkart, and Margo Okazawa-Rey. Washington, DC: Network of Educators, 1998. 77–80.

McDowell, Deborah. "New Direction for Black Feminist Criticism." *Black American Literature Forum* 14.4 (Winter 1980): 153–59.

McKay, Claude. *Home to Harlem*. Boston: Northeastern UP, 1928.

Milliken, Stephen. *Chester Himes: A Critical Appraisal*. Columbia: U of Missouri P, 1976.

Morrison, Toni. "Unspeakable Things Unspoken: The Afro-American Presence in American Literature." In *Within the Circle*. Ed. Angelyn Mitchell. Durham: Duke UP, 1994. 368–98.

———. *Sula*. New York: Penguin, 1973.

———. "The Official Story: Dead Man Golfing." In *Birth of a Nation'hood: Gaze, Script, and Spectacle in the O. J. Simpson Case*. Ed. Toni Morrison and Claudia Brodsky Lacour. New York: Random House, 1997. vii–xxviii.

———. *Paradise*. New York: Random House, 1997.

———. *Beloved*. New York: Penguin Books, 1987.

Mosley, Walter. *Always, Outnumbered, Always Outgunned*. New York: Washington Square, 1998.

———. "Giving Back." In *Black Genius: African American Solutions to African American Problems*. Ed. Walter Mosley, Manthia Diawara, Clyde Taylor, and Regina Austin. New York: W. W. Norton, 1999.

———. *Walkin' the Dog*. Boston: Back Bay, 1999.

Muller, Gilbert. *Chester Himes*. Boston: Twayne, 1989.

Smith, Barbara. "Toward a Black Feminist Criticism." In *All the Women Are White and All the Blacks Are Men, but Some of Us Are Brave*. Ed. Gloria T. Hull, Patricia Bell Scott, and Barbara Smith. New York: Feminist Press, 1982. 157–75.

Smith, Valerie. "Gender and Afro-Americanist Literary Theory and Criticism." In *Within the Circle*. Ed. Angelyn Mitchell. Durham: Duke UP, 1994. 482–98.

Stanford, Ann Folwell. "He Speaks for Whom? Inscription and Reinscription of Women in *Invisible Man* and *The Salt Eaters*." *MELUS* 18.2 (Summer 1993): 17–31.

Walker, Alice. *The Third Life of Grange Copeland*. New York: Pocket Books, 1970.

Werner, Craig Hansen. *Paradoxical Resolutions: American Fiction since James Joyce*. Urbana: U of Illinois P, 1982.

Williams, Sherley Anne. "Papa Dick and Sister-Woman: Reflections on Women in the Fiction of Richard Wright." In *American Novelists Revisited: Essays in Feminist Criticism*. Ed. Fritz Fleischmann. Boston: G. K. Hall, 1982. 394–415.

Wright, Richard. *Native Son*. New York: HarperPerennial, 1940.

Index

agency, of black women, 20, 22; as emasculating to black men, 37. *See also* social agency

Ali, Muhammad, 109

Always Outnumbered, Always Outgunned (Mosley), 26; black male feminist framework of, 136, 137, 171; black manhood and institutional racism in, 141; essentialist perspective on blackness in, 153–54; and the idea of a divine plan for Socrates, 145–46; and "implosive victimization," 142, 145, 146–48, 155, 157; Lavant Hall in, 155, 156; moral and cultural politics of Socrates in, 144, 151–53; Mr. and Mrs. Minette in, 145–46; police activity and relation to black-on-black abuse in, 142–43, 152; problem of social implementation in, 150–51; Proctor in, 149, 150; racial biases of Bruce Tynan in, 152–53; resistance to oppression and the example of the Capricorn bookstores in, 144–45; Right Burke in, 142, 143; short-story structure of, 140; slavery imagery in, 151–52; Socrates and the fate of Petis in, 135–36, 151,

152; Socrates' mentoring of Darryl in, 140–42, 144; Stoney in, 154; and violence as a mechanism of resistance, 152; thematic significance of the arsonist's suicide in, 154–55; and violence as a mechanism of resistance, 152, 158; white philanthropy in, 149–50; Young Africans group in, 143–44

Autobiography of Miss Jane Pittman, The (Gaines), 4

Awkward, Michael, 10, 13, 14, 19–20, 29, 35; on black women and self-sacrifice, 122–23; critique of *Sula* by, 20–22

"Back to Africa" movement, 85

Baker, Houston, 10

Baldwin, James, 24–25, 159, 175; contributions of to the black male feminist project, 64–69, 78–79; and criticism of his gender politics, 49; views of on theory and categories, 53

Bambara, Toni Cade, 25–26, 105–6, 138; feminist politics of, 107–10; on gender-racial liberation, 109–10; on gender tensions in the black community, 107–8

Baraka, Amiri, 11–13
Beloved (Morrison), 3, 81, 171
biological determinism, 15
Black Arts Movement, 11, 12
"Black Feminist Statement, A" (Smith, Smith, and Frazier), 15
Black Genius: African American Solutions to African American Problems (ed. Mosley), 137
"Black Man's Place(s) in Black Feminist Criticism, A" (Awkward), 19–20
black masculinity / manhood, 6, 20, 47, 49, 52, 81, 150, 174–75; as an act of sexual domination, 87–88; and the black man–white woman murder taboo, 86; and the erasure of black women's desires, 20; and gender dynamics, 22; and pathologies of self-hatred, 85; and relation between black manhood and complicity, 147–48; stereotyped views of, 123. *See also Always Outnumbered, Always Outgunned* (Mosley): black manhood and institutional racism in
black men, 122, 175; cultural fragmentation of, 159–60; and the gender politics of black male texts, 47; social progress of, 44–45. *See also* black masculinity / manhood; black patriarchy
black nationalism, 7, 32, 82; discourse of, 105–6
"blackness," 139
black patriarchy, 2, 3, 20, 23, 103–4; black female complicity in, 5, 64–65, 116; cultural variables reinforcing, 27; dismantling of, 47, 103; ending of, 22; problems of across gender lines, 78–79; and the psychological traumas of slavery, 97; resis-

tance to, 77–78; victim status as the premise of, 4
black primitivism, 86
black suffering: discourse of, 2; necessary versus unnecessary, 113–15, 121; and treatment of female suffering in black-authored texts, 5–6; white identification with, 12
Black Woman, The (Bambara), 107–10; gender tensions within, 107–8; and the rejection of white gender roles, 108–9
black women, 3–4, 14–15, 50, 52, 122, 175; black male disregard for, 11; erasure of in white women's writing, 18; as "evil matriarchs," 109; failings of, 164; and the "myth of the strong black woman," 116–17, 119; and the pressure of self-sacrifice, 122–23; subjugation of within and outside the black community, 106–7. *See also* black suffering
Black Women in the Fiction of James Baldwin (Harris), 49
blues, the, 139; anger, and the "false blues," 138–39
Bouson, J. Brooks, 84–85
Butler-Evans, Elliott, 14, 106, 107
butterfly effect, 161
Byerman, Keith, 116

Carbado, Devon W., 14, 87; on dismantling of gender taboos, 123; on "unmodified antiracist discourse," 122
Carby, Hazel, 13; criticism of black feminism, 17–18; politics of, 18
"Change the Joke and Slip the Yoke" (Ellison), 129
Chesnutt, Charles, 6, 47
Christian, Barbara, 14
class, 18, 30

Go Tell It on the Mountain (Baldwin)
(continued)
complicity of black women in patriarchy, 64–65, 68, 69, 74, 77;
"conversion" of John in, 76–77; as
a critique of gender politics, 52–53;
Deborah in, 60–61; disruption of
the victimization discourse in, 50;
and the dynamic of erasure in, 73;
and the effect of black patriarchy on
women in, 50–51, 63–64; Elizabeth
in, 50–51, 53; Elizabeth's spiritual
crisis in, 65–66; fallout between
Gabriel and Roy in, 59–60; Florence
in, 25, 51, 53; Florence's exposure
of Gabriel as an adulterer in, 76–77;
Gabriel in, 49, 52–53; and Gabriel's
betrayal of Deborah in, 74–76; and
Gabriel's idea of himself as a victim
in, 56, 61–63; and Gabriel's mother
as the model of ideal black womanhood, 55; and Gabriel's response to
Roy's injuries, 53–54; John in, 51,
73, 74, 76–77; lack of closure in,
76; mistreatment of women by Gabriel in, 55–56, 57; models of black
female resistance to patriarchy in,
77–78; patriarchal entitlement in,
55, 73–75; patriarchal theology of
Gabriel in, 57; political evolution
of Florence in, 69–75; preoccupation of Gabriel with Elizabeth's sin
in, 56–57, 62–63; and the problem
of victim status in, 53–54, 60–63,
67–68; relationship of Esther and
Richard in, 65–67; relationship of
Florence and Gabriel in, 73–75;
relationship of Florence with God
in, 69, 71–73, 77; relationship of
Gabriel and Esther in, 61–64; Richard's suicide in, 53; significance of

Florence's return to the church in,
68–69; social standing of Esther in,
63–64

"Harlem is Nowhere" (Ellison), 159
Harris, Trudier, 2, 14, 53; and criticism of James Baldwin, 49, 52
"He Speaks for Whom? Inscription
and Reinscription of Women in *Invisible Man* and *The Salt Eaters*"
(Stanford), 106–7
Hill-Collins, Patricia, 14
Himes, Chester, 24; accusations
against black women and white men
by, 42; misogynist attitudes of, 31–
32; monist politics of, 43
Hogness, Peter, 142
Home to Harlem (McKay), 9–10
hooks, bell, 14, 116–17; on martyrdom, 120; on the "surrogate oppressor," 120
Hurston, Zora Neale, 58, 118

If He Hollers Let Him Go (Himes),
24, 29–30; black male feminist perspective of, 46–47; and the black
middle class, 30–31; black women
as political props in, 49–50; Bob
Jones as a "modern day Everyman,"
24, 30, 31, 40; Bob Jones' compromise of his integrity for social
status in, 36–37; Bob Jones' "crisis" of masculinity in, 33–36; Bob
Jones' preoccupation with whiteness in, 37; Bob Jones' relationship
and characterization of Ella Mae in,
32–33; Bob Jones' relationship with
Madge in, 45–46; Bob Jones' views
of the black middle class, 39–40;
class issues involved in Bob Jones'
relationship with Alice, 30, 35–40,

Neale, Mark Anthony, 14
"New Directions for Black Feminist
Criticism" (McDowell), 15–16
Notes of a Native Son (Baldwin), 53

"Official Story, The: Dead Man Golfing" (Morrison), 22
oppression, of blacks, 11, 22, 133,
164; black complicity in, 23, 139–
40; and black "innocence," 157; of
black men, 12–13; of black women,
4, 40–41, 122–23; formidability of,
138; as a master narrative for understanding social issues, 166; and
the oppression/oppressor distinction, 137–38; racial binaries involved in, 5, 138, 148–50; and "surrogate" oppressors, 5, 120. *See also*
oppression, resistance to
oppression, resistance to, 46, 138; and
the blues as a form of resistance,
139; and limitations of resistance
strategies premised on blame, 160–
61. See also *Always Outnumbered,*
Always Outgunned (Mosley): and
violence as a mechanism of
resistance
Oxherding Tale (Johnson), 4

"Papa Dick and Sister-Woman: Reflections on Women in the Fiction of
Richard Wright" (Williams), 2–3
Paradise (Morrison), 25, 81, 164,
165; and alternatives to patriarchy
in, 96–97; Arnold and Jeff Fleetwood in, 86, 92, 93; black man–
white woman murder taboo in, 86–
87; and black masculinity as an act
of sexual domination, 87–88; Connie in, 82, 102; Connie's reaction to
her power to resurrect the dead in,
99–100; critique of black patriarchy
in, 103–4; critique of white supremacist ideology in, 85; Deacon (Deek)
Morgan in, 81–82, 83–84, 85, 86,
90, 92, 95–96, 102–3; and "the
Disallowing," 84–85, 94–95, 97,
98; Elder Morgan in, 96; eulogy of
Reverend Misner for Save-Maria in,
101–2; exploitative financial practice of the Morgan twins in, 95–96;
Harper and Menus Jury in, 86, 91–
92, 93; and the image of women as
prey in, 89, 90; and the importance
of discarded knowledge in the black
community, 90–91; and the internalization of white supremacy in,
94, 95, 96, 101, 103–4; interrogation of black masculinity in, 85–86;
K.D. in, 84, 92; Lone Dupres in,
90–91, 92–93; murder of the white
woman as the ultimate act of black
male liberation in, 87–88, 93; plot
summation of, 82–84; problematic
relationship of Connie and Deek
in, 100–101; problematic relationship of Connie and Mary Magna in,
98–100, 101; and the reconceptual-
ization of black manhood in, 96–97;
relationship of black patriarchy and
white supremacy in, 93–95, 98; resistance of the convent women to
male violence in, 93; response of the
town of Ruby to the attack on the
convent in, 103–4; Reverend Misner
in, 82, 95, 96, 101–2; and the Ruby
men's conception of 8-rock womanhood, 89–90; and the Ruby men's
justifications for slaying the convent
women, 88–89, 91–92; Sargeant
Person in, 86, 92; and the sexual
politics involved in the Ruby men's